David Hare

Behind the Beautiful Forevers

David Hare is the author of thirty full-length plays for the stage, seventeen of which have been presented at the National Theatre. They include *Slag*, *The Great Exhibition*, *Brassneck* (with Howard Brenton), *Knuckle*, *Fanshen*, *Teeth 'n' Smiles*, *Plenty*, *A Map of the World*, *Pravda* (with Howard Brenton), *The Bay at Nice*, *The Secret Rapture*, *Racing Demon*, *Murmuring Judges*, *The Absence of War*, *Skylight*, *Amy's View*, *The Blue Room* (from Schnitzler), *The Judas Kiss*, *Via Dolorosa*, *My Zinc Bed*, *The Breath of Life*, *The Permanent Way*, *Stuff Happens*, *The Vertical Hour*, *Gethsemane*, *Berlin/Wall*, *The Power of Yes* and *South Downs*. His many screenplays for film and television include *Licking Hitler*, *Wetherby*, *Damage*, *The Hours*, *The Reader*, *Page Eight*, *Turks & Caicos* and *Salting the Battlefield*. He has also written English adaptations of plays by Brecht, Gorky, Chekhov, Pirandello, Ibsen and Lorca.

Behind
the
Beautiful
Forevers

— A PLAY BY —

David
Hare

Based on the book by Katherine Boo

FARRAR, STRAUS AND GIROUX

NEW YORK

Farrar, Straus and Giroux
120 Broadway, New York 10271

Originally published in 2014 by Faber and Faber Ltd., Great Britain
Revised edition originally published in 2015 by
Faber and Faber Ltd., Great Britain
Published in the United States by Farrar, Straus and Giroux
First American edition, 2015

Library of Congress Cataloging-in-Publication Data
Hare, David, 1947–
    Behind the beautiful forevers : a play / by David Hare. — First American
edition.
        pages ; cm
    "Based on the book by Katherine Boo."
    ISBN 978-0-86547-835-0 (softcover) — ISBN 978-0-374-71409-3 (ebook)
    1. Urban poor—India—Mumbai—Drama. I. Boo, Katherine. Behind
the beautiful forevers. II. Title.

PR6058.A678 B44 2015
822'.914—dc23

                                                                2015022199

Our books may be purchased in bulk for promotional, educational, or
business use. Please contact your local bookseller or the Macmillan
Corporate and Premium Sales Department at 1-800-221-7945, extension
5442, or by e-mail at MacmillanSpecialMarkets@macmillan.com.

www.fsgbooks.com
www.twitter.com/fsgbooks • www.facebook.com/fsgbooks

P1

Behind the Beautiful Forevers, produced in association with Scott Rudin, was first performed in the Olivier auditorium of the National Theatre, London, on 10 November 2014. The cast was as follows:

Sunil Sharma Hiran Abeysekera
Deepak Rai *aka* **Kalu** Assad Zaman
Manju Waghekar Anjana Vasan
Asha Waghekar Stephanie Street
Abdul Husain Shane Zaza
Raja Kamble Ranjit Krishnamma
Mahadeo Waghekar Sartaj Garewal
Rahul Waghekar Gavi Singh Chera
Zehrunisa Husain Meera Syal
Kehkashan Husain Anjli Mohindra
Karam Husain Vincent Ebrahim
Sub-Inspector Shankar Yeram *aka* **Fish-Lips**
    Chook Sibtain
Nagare Muzz Khan
Fatima Shaikh *aka* **One Leg** Thusitha Jayasundera
Mirchi Husain Ronak Patani
Meena Chinnu Anneika Rose
Airport Director Sartaj Garewal
Cynthia Ali Manjeet Mann
Officer Kulkarni Mariam Haque
Laxmi Chinnu Bharti Patel
Noori Shaikh Tia-Lana Chinapyel / Nikita Mehta /
    Tia Palamathanan
Abdul Shaikh Ranjit Krishnamma
Poornima Paikrao Nathalie Armin
Guard at Dongri Esh Alladi

The Master Pal Aron
Taufeeq Muzz Khan
Judge P. M. Chauhan Thusitha Jayasundera
Clerk of the Court Mariam Haque
Defender Esh Alladi
Prosecutor Chook Sibtain
Judge C. K. Dhiran Pal Aron

All other parts played by members of the Company

Director Rufus Norris
Designer Katrina Lindsay
Lighting Designer Paule Constable
Sound Designer Paul Arditti

Characters

in order of appearance

Sunil Sharma
twelve

Deepak Rai *aka* **Kalu**
fifteen

Manju Waghekar
Asha's daughter, eighteen

Abdul Husain
maybe sixteen

Asha Waghekar

Raja Kamble

Mahadeo Waghekar
Asha's husband

Rahul Waghekar
fifteen

Zehrunisa Husain
Abdul's mother

Kehkashan Husain
Zehrunisa's daughter, nineteen

Karam Husain
Zehrunisa's husband

Sub-Inspector Shankar Yeram *aka* **Fish-Lips**

Officer Nagare

Fatima Shaikh *aka* **One Leg**

Mirchi Husain
Abdul's brother, fourteen

Meena Chinnu
fifteen

Airport Director

Cynthia Ali
a neighbour

Officer Kulkarni

Laxmi Chinnu
Meena's mother

Noori Shaikh
eight

Abdul Shaikh
Fatima's husband

Poornima Paikrao
Special Executive Officer

The Guard

The Master

Taufeeq

Judge P. M. Chauhan

Clerk of the Court

Defender

Prosecutor

Judge C. K. Dhiran

Dealers, Pickers, Doctors, Police, Guards,
Prisoners, Detainees, Neighbours

The play is set in and around Annawadi,
Mumbai, 2008–2009

Behind
the
Beautiful
Forevers

Act One

A bare stage, epic. It's a maidan, as yet undefined. Abdul Husain comes on. He is in his late teens, wiry, sullen – an old man of a boy. He has a matchstick between his teeth. Behind him there is a huge mound of mixed rubbish and a rusty pair of scales hangs from a roof. Sunil Sharma arrives. He's twelve, cheerful, very short, with a thick upward pelt of hair. He carries a large sack of rubbish. He speaks directly to us.

Sunil Know what I want? I want cotton buds. I want ketchup packets. Because silver paper is good. Chocolate. Cigarettes. Cigarette packets. Umbrellas. That's what I want. Cardboard. Plastic. Batteries. Shoelaces. Metal. Problem: there's always a wall. Wherever you go, you'll find a new wall. With barbed wire, or bottled glass. All the time, new guards, new dogs, new guns. There's a lot of good stuff in the world, that's why they've electrified the fences. Who's been to the airport? Mumbai airport? Anybody? It's not just that rich people don't know what they've got. They don't even know what they throw away. They don't notice. We notice. The airport's bigger every day. That's why there's more of us. Picking garbage. Me, I'm always searching for a place. I don't know where it is, but I know it's there. Beyond Airport Road. It must be. Somewhere, there's a place full of rubbish no one else has thought of.

1.2

At the back of the stage a concrete wall, covered by sunshine-yellow ads for Italianate floor tiles. Along its whole length, the repeated words BEAUTIFUL FOREVER

3

BEAUTIFUL FOREVER BEAUTIFUL FOREVER. *At once Sunil is joined by Kalu, who is fifteen, on a motorbike, in camouflage cargo-pants, dark-skinned, with long, lank hair. Abdul is sorting his pile of rubbish.*

Kalu Sunil, are you coming out? Are you coming out with me tonight?

Sunil does not answer.

What's happening, man? What, you don't want to make money?

Sunil I want to make money.

Kalu Then why aren't you coming, man? You want to pick plastic all your life?

Sunil smiles in anticipation.

Sunil Kalu, do *Om Shanti Om*.

Kalu No.

Sunil Please.

Kalu Come out with me, I'll do *Om Shanti Om*. Fuck, I'll do *Bhool Bhulaiya*. I'll do *King Kong*. I'll do fucking Bruce Lee if that's what you want. I'll do the whole lot if you'll just help.

Kalu looks a moment. Then he does a beautiful brief parody of Deepika sashaying in Om Shanti Om.

Well?

He shakes his head.

Oh I see, so you're scared, are you, man?

Sunil I'm not scared.

Kalu Scared of ghosts?

Sunil I'm not scared of ghosts. I go out at night.

Kalu It's sitting there. The stuff is sitting there, man. In the recycling bins.

Sunil How did you find it?

Kalu I have contacts. They told me where it was.

Sunil They told you? Somebody told you where to find metal? Why would they do that? You're lying, man.

Kalu It's over by the airport. Where they fix the planes. Up over the wire and we're in.

Sunil finally tells him the reason.

Sunil Kalu, you look like a thief.

Kalu I am a thief.

Sunil They can tell. The airport people can tell. They take one look in your eyes. Once you get a thief-face you're finished. I don't want that face.

Kalu What about you? You look like a runt. You look like a stub. How can you bear being so small?

Sunil My father was a picker. I'm a picker. Thieves are different.

Kalu Tell you how we're different. We make a living. That's how we're different. There's no future in plastic. Metal – that's where the money is. Tonight, I'll do the job, then I'll go to Noodle-wali, eat chilli chicken and rice. Isn't that what you want? To eat chilli chicken and rice? You really saying no?

Abdul looks up.

Abdul He's saying no.

Kalu Abdul you're a prick. You handle stolen goods all day, but you don't have the balls to go and get them.

Abdul I'm not a picker. I'm a sorter.

Sunil Yes. But I'm a garbage picker. I'm not a thief.

Kalu gets on his motorbike and goes.

Sunil opens his trash sack to check its contents. Manju Waghekar is in line, with a pail of water. Behind, a queue of women with buckets at a spluttering standpipe. Manju is tall, poised, eighteen, at ease with her beauty. She speaks to us.

Manju *Mrs Dalloway*. I don't understand it. It's a book by the English writer Virginia Woolf. Do you understand it? Who are these people? What do they do? I know nothing of these people. I try to read it. Clarissa goes out to get flowers. Later she gives a party. I'm trying to learn it, that's my only chance, I'm going to learn it by heart.

From offstage, the sound of Manju's mother, Asha, calling for her.

Asha (*off*) Manju!

Manju It's not easy. When I read, my mind slips down the page. The First World War, I know about that, I've heard of that. But the rest. And like why she wrote the book, why we should care.

Asha (*off*) Manju!

Manju In books I've read before, there's always a story. I'm looking for a story.

Asha (*off*) Manju! Where are you? Come here. What's happened to you?

Manju If there were a story, it would be easier to learn.

1.4

Sunil goes over to Abdul with his sack.

Sunil Abdul.

Abdul Sunil.

Sunil Are you going to weigh it?

Abdul takes the sack and puts it on the scales.

There's enough here we can go to the video parlour.

Abdul says nothing.

Abdul, you have to do something besides work. Come play Bomber-Man. Come play Metal Slug Three.

Abdul If I don't work the family don't eat.

Sunil You're making more money than any of us. Everyone knows. The Husains are doing well.

Abdul pulls out a sheaf of rupees.

Hey, put it on again, I didn't see.

Abdul But I saw.

Sunil Yeah. But I didn't.

Abdul reluctantly puts the bag back on the scales. Meanwhile:

You never have fun. You never get high.

Abdul I work. There's eleven in my family. That's what I do. What do I tell you? What's the first rule? What is it?

Sunil / Abdul (*mockingly, together*) 'Keep your head down, keep out of trouble . . .'

Sunil So you keep saying.

Abdul Keep out of trouble. It's the only rule.

Sunil You're too cautious.

Abdul And you're too flashy, Sunil. It's good to be careful. Because it only takes one thing. Just one.

He has raised his voice, in absolute conviction.

Sunil I know what you are. You're a coward. You're frightened. You're frightened of life.

Abdul So what if I'm a coward? I stay alive, don't I?

He hands over the rupees.

Sunil Thank you. Is that it?

Abdul That's it.

Sunil That's good stuff.

Abdul It's all good stuff.

Sunil I thought I'd get more. I thought you'd pay me more.

He waits a moment, as if to bring pressure.

Abdul.

Abdul Then bring more.

1.5

Sunil goes. Abdul carries on sorting garbage, with breathtaking speed and skill. Upstage, Glimmerglass hotels shimmer behind the wall. They become a permanent background, towering over the action. Asha Waghekar appears. She's thirty-nine, imperious, used to power. She addresses us.

Asha Five hotels. In Annawadi, we live under five hotels. They built walls so the guests wouldn't have to look at us, so the guests wouldn't know we were here. But every night the ash from our cow-dung fires drifts across and lands on their swimming pools. They complain. The world is changing, and it's changing fast. It's tipping eastwards and the money is flowing this way. Globalisation. But the politicians are unhappy. Mumbai's doing well but Singapore and Shanghai are doing better. Why? Because Mumbai doesn't seem modern. Why not? Obvious. Because of us. Here we are, sitting in the way beside the airport, stopping the economic miracle being a miracle.

8

We have that. At least we have that. The fact they want to get rid of us. That's our power. That's the only power we have. All anyone wants to know: when will we finally get out the way?

1.6

Asha sits. Outside, an orderly and silent queue has formed, waiting to see her. In another area, Abdul continues to sort rubbish. Manju comes in, carrying her pail of water.

Asha Manju, ah, there you are at last. I've been waiting. Where were you?

Manju The tap's dry again. I stood for three hours.

Asha You can study at the tap.

Manju I did study. I took *Mrs Dalloway*.

She gives a withering look, then goes to wash vegetables.

There's already a queue.

Asha The longer they wait, the more they appreciate it when they do get to see me.

Manju crosses to go out to the queue.

Manju Mr Kamble's waiting. I don't think he should wait.

Asha Why not?

Manju You know why not.

Raja Kamble is at the head of the queue. He's only forty, but in terrible condition, knobbly, bony, a mouthful of yellowed teeth.

Mr Kamble, please, you must come in. I know my mother will want to help.

9

Kamble Thank you, Manju. You're a good girl. How are your studies?

Manju Good. Come in.

He smiles and moves across to see Asha. Manju works quietly at the side.

Asha Raja.

Kamble Asha. I'm here to ask for your help.

Asha makes a gesture for him to proceed.

You know my situation.

Asha Tell me.

Kamble Not good. I need a new valve for my heart.

Asha What's the doctor asking? For himself?

Kamble He won't do it for less than sixty thousand rupees.

Asha Which hospital?

Kamble Sion.

Asha Have you tried Cooper?

Kamble He wants more.

He looks at her, calculating.

I need money. I've heard there's a government scheme . . .

Asha Ah yes.

Kamble And you can fix it. You're the go-to woman. You fix things for the party.

Asha I work with Shiv Sena, yes.

Kamble People, they get given money to start small businesses.

Asha Some people.

Kamble It's you who decides. It's you who fills in the forms saying how many people the business employs. It's you who cooks up the figure.

Asha looks at him, her look unyielding.

Asha It's an anti-poverty scheme. It's a government initiative. To help people to help themselves.

Kamble Well?

Asha hesitates. Manju has stopped working and is looking to see what will happen.

Asha How much do you need?

Kamble I'm forty thousand short. Asha, look at me. Without this valve, I will die.

Asha is impassive.

You and I, our families have been friends. Since we first came here. Manju's like my daughter. At the sanitation department, I'm respected.

Asha You clean toilets.

Kamble Yes.

Asha You're a toilet cleaner.

Kamble I have a permanent job. I was born on the pavement and now, because of toilets, my family live in brick walls. Asha, if you could get me forty, I would be able to make a token of thanks.

Asha What would this token be?

Kamble I will give you five thousand.

Asha Five? You'd give me five?

She waits. Kamble nods. Then:

Pray.

Kamble What?

Asha Pray to the gods, man. You're in a bad way. Go to the temple. Go to Gajanan Maharaj and offer a prayer.

Kamble A prayer for what?

Asha For whatever you want. Pray for money, or pray for good health. At the moment you need both.

Manju Mother, you can't let him go. You can't. This is Mr Kamble. He's a family friend.

Asha Manju, this is not your business.

Manju It's wrong. You know it's wrong.

Asha Be quiet.

Manju has spoken out in agony. But Asha slaps her down fiercely. She turns back to Kamble.

You think fixing is easy?

Kamble No.

Asha People come, they say 'Give me a loan'. Do you know how many people come to me? It's not a tap. Yes, I'm a friend, and as a friend, I say 'Pray to the gods'. Thank you for coming to see me.

Kamble Asha . . .

Asha Thank you. That's it.

It's final. Kamble goes out. Manju moves vegetables into a pot. Asha fumes.

I won't have it. I won't have you speaking when I'm working.

Manju busies herself, saying nothing.

Come on, he's a dying man. He'll pay more than five. I'm his only hope. Look. Learn. Understand what I do. It's not clever to be stupid. I brought you up wrong. You think because he's a friend, I should treat him differently? One day I want to be corporator. You think I'll get to run the ward by being kind? Who was kind to me when the crops died and there was no food? When we lived in Vidharba, the girl children all starved. So many years and I can still taste it. The taste of hunger in my mouth. Now you study, you teach. Why? Because I gave you what my family refused to give me. Because I was a girl. What's the book you're reading?

Manju *Mrs Dalloway*.

Asha Yes. You think I read *Mrs Dalloway*? In the country? I was skin and bone. I wanted you to be sweet, but instead you're soft.

Mahadeo comes in, gentle, fleshy, fifties. With him Rahul, fifteen, in cargo-pants, snaggle-toothed, pie-faced, with long flowing locks.

Mahadeo Is supper ready?

Asha It's late. Because your daughter was late.

Rahul (*to Manju*) Are you in trouble again?

Asha As usual. If she had a proper father this wouldn't happen.

Mahadeo It isn't my fault.

Asha Everything's your fault.

Mahadeo Is there a drink anywhere?

Mahadeo gives Manju a complicit smile.

Asha Mr Kamble was here. He offered me five. He'll come back. He'll offer more. Where else can he go? He doesn't want to die.

The stage changes. It's night. A wire fence. Arc lights. It's the red and white gates of an Air India compound. The gates are open. The place is deserted. Kalu arrives, clearly expecting someone. He goes through the gate. He looks round.

Kalu Who's that?

Silence.

Who's there?

There's a sound. Kalu begins to panic and turns. Two Dealers in white suits appear from the dark.

First Dealer Kalu.

Kalu backs away towards the gate, but the Second Dealer is already there, slamming it shut with a big metallic crash.

Take off his shirt.

The Second Dealer moves to take hold of Kalu while the First Dealer takes off his own jacket.

You're going to lose your eyes.

Kalu Let me go. I haven't done anything. I've done nothing. I've done nothing wrong.

The Second Dealer has torn off Kalu's shirt, holding him from behind. The First Dealer has a dagger in one hand and a sickle in the other.

First Dealer You work for the police.

Kalu No, I don't.

First Dealer Yes, you do.

Kalu I haven't told anyone anything.

The Second Dealer readies his body. The First Dealer raises the dagger.

First Dealer Kalu. You're going to die.

The First Dealer stabs Kalu in the eye. Blood spurts. Kalu screams. From the back of the theatre the sound of an approaching plane. The First Dealer stabs again, then pulls the eye out with his hand. A massive shadow moves across as a 747 passes low overhead, lights flashing. Then the jet disappears.

1.8

Abdul is sitting exactly where he was, sorting rubbish with spectacular skill. There is a line of Pickers waiting patiently. Zehrunisa Husain has appeared. She is maybe forty, a little plump but light in her movements.

Zehrunisa I can't help it. We're doing better. We're doing better than other people. So what? It's not our fault. And yet everyone dislikes us. What can we do? Abdul's the best sorter in the district. My dullest son, Abdul, and the hardest working. Three years ago, the monsoon came, Annawadi was under water and we lost everything. But we started again, we rebuilt. Now it's all good news. The Chinese have the Olympics, they have to build, so there's more demand. More demand for everything, rubbish included. They do well, we all do well. We don't eat weeds and we don't fry rats. My husband has an idea. He's bought a plot of land ninety minutes from here. At Vasai. Just land, nothing else. There, it's all Muslims. So nobody talks about 'dirty Muslim money'. But if we go, he'll have me back behind a burqa, serving tea. Fuck that. Never. Never again.

She turns to a Picker who is waiting.

Ten. That's all you're getting. Come and check behind me, you see me shitting coins? Go home and suck on your husband's sugar cane.

The Picker goes, discontented. Scenery appears. Elements of a shack. A couple of walls, a window, and an entrance. Kehkashan is nineteen, capable but moody. Zehrunisa joins her, and the two of them wash clothes, squatting together as Abdul goes on sorting.

Kehkashan When do you want lunch?

Zehrunisa Later. And don't mope anymore, it's enough. There's nothing you can do.

Kehkashan I'm not going back. I'm not going back to him.

Zehrunisa throws an anxious look towards Abdul.

Zehrunisa Move away, Abdul, I don't want you to hear this.

Abdul Move away where exactly?

Zehrunisa Your sister's not happy.

Kehkashan Of course I'm not happy. Why would I be happy? Abdul can listen, I've nothing to hide.

Abdul chews the plastic with his teeth to test it.

Abdul If there's anything I hate it's bottle-tops. Half plastic, half metal. You cut your hands to pieces pulling them apart. And for what?

Zehrunisa For our future, Abdul. To get us out of here. Isn't that what you want?

Abdul throws his mother a sardonic glance.

What? What are you saying? You don't want to leave?

Abdul We make a living. It's not so bad.

Zehrunisa There's a market in people just like there's a market in rubbish. And Muslims in rubbish come bottom of the pile. I'd like to live somewhere where people don't hate us.

Abdul smiles, unfazed.

Abdul They don't even notice us.

Zehrunisa They notice your sister. Men around her like flies.

Kehkashan That's not my fault.

Zehrunisa I didn't say it was your fault.

Kehkashan is shaking her head.

Kehkashan I'm not going back, why should I? Explain to me, please, why I should stay with a man, I should stay with a man who has photos of another woman . . .

Zehrunisa Kehkashan, please . . .

Kehkashan Intimate photos . . .

Zehrunisa All right . . .

Kehkashan Intimate photos on his mobile phone?

Zehrunisa turns at once to Abdul.

Zehrunisa Abdul, close your ears.

Abdul No.

Zehrunisa You don't need to hear this.

Abdul I've heard it already.

Zehrunisa Abdul . . .

Abdul At least fifty times.

Kehkashan Why should I stay with a man like that? Why should I have to?

There is a moment.

Zehrunisa You've been hurt. You've been badly hurt.

Kehkashan shakes her head, unhappy.

Kehkashan I didn't choose him, remember? You chose him. You chose him for me when I was two!

Zehrunisa So? He was a fucking good match.

Kehkashan A good match?

Zehrunisa Yes.

Kehkashan He was my cousin.

Zehrunisa That's what I said, a good match.

Kehkashan Only nobody bothered to tell me: he had another woman all along.

Zehrunisa I didn't know.

Kehkashan What, I'm meant to put up with that? A husband who ignores me, who spends all his time with somebody else?

She is overwhelmed. She turns away.

You ordered me to love him. I loved him. But I couldn't make him love me.

Zehrunisa and Abdul work on.

And your language is unacceptable.

Zehrunisa Fuck my language.

Kehkashan From a woman.

Zehrunisa It's what I've got. It's what I need. I'll speak like a rattlesnake and if it scares people so much the better. 'I'm scared of the mother,' the pickers say. It's good for business. A bad tongue is a good strategy.

She smiles.

Now we need to find Abdul a wife.

Abdul Oh sure.

Zehrunisa Don't you want a wife?

Abdul I want a wife who doesn't say 'pimp' or 'motherfucker'.

He stops work a moment.

I hear this word 'love' so often. I think I know it, but I don't feel it. And I don't know why.

Zehrunisa You will feel it.

Karam, forties, appears, breathy, feeble, his lungs wheezing. He is in a blue-check lunghi, with an Urdu newspaper under his arm.

Oh, so he's back. Work not too hard for you, I hope?

Karam You know full well: I'm ill.

Zehrunisa How far away are the riots?

Karam I don't know exactly. That way and turn right.

He waves an airy hand.

Zehrunisa How far did they get?

Karam Well short of the airport. Is lunch ready?

Zehrunisa looks at him contemptuously. Kehkashan turns and goes indoors.

Don't look at me like that. They're miles away. They won't come near us.

Zehrunisa Why not? We're Muslims, aren't we? If they come this way, we're fucked.

Karam So? So many things can fuck us. Bollywood's already fucking us with their stupid clean-up campaign. Great big film stars on great big billboards, grinning at us: 'Don't drop litter.' What sort of message is that? If people don't drop litter, we're dead. I tear down those posters whenever I see them.

Zehrunisa Good for you.

Karam These new trucks. Terrible. Driving down the centre of the road, picking up everything. 'Clean up the city!' Hey – d'you mind, that's our job, that's our livelihood.

Zehrunisa laughs.

Zehrunisa You should go into politics.

Karam I might just do that.

Zehrunisa Stand for prime minister?

Karam Later. One step at a time.

Sunil appears, petrified, a long way off. Abdul at once knows something terrible has happened.

Abdul Mother, can you go in? Please. I'm asking. Please.

Everyone goes inside. The boys alone.

Sunil It's Kalu.

Abdul I knew it.

Sunil He's dead.

Abdul I knew this would happen. What did I say? What did I always say?

Sunil He had a sickle up his arse. They ripped out his arsehole. They fed his eyes to the birds.

Abdul Where is he?

He raises his voice.

Where is he?

Sunil Don't go. The police have got him.

Abdul I'm asking where he is.

Sunil It happened at the airport.

Abdul Where?

Sunil In the garden.

Abdul Which garden? It's all gardens. Since the airport got taken over, it's nothing but stupid gardens!

Sunil By the Air India gates.

Abdul is hysterical. He moves, as if to set off.

Abdul, don't go!

Abdul stops.

Abdul Who did it?

Sunil Nobody knows. The people he was meeting.

Abdul Dealers?

Sunil Maybe. Maybe police. Maybe guards. The police are rounding everyone up. All the pickers. They're taking us in. We're all under suspicion.

Abdul Suspicion of what?

Sunil Who cares? It's an excuse! They can do what they want!

Abdul moves away, by himself. He is crying.

Abdul Kalu. I don't believe it. Kalu.

1.10

The gates of Air India. Kalu's body has been covered in muslin and laid out on a stretcher on the ground. Sub-Inspector Shankar Yeram, aka Fish-Lips, with a distinctive mouth, speaks to us.

Fish-Lips Figures. Everyone's obsessed with figures. Statistics. Targets. Meet your target. For an experienced officer, there's one rule. Never classify anything as murder. Call it what you like but you don't call it murder. It spoils the statistics. This district has the best clear-up rate in Mumbai. We only had two murders last year and both cleared up. One hundred percent detection rate. We got a certificate, we got a bonus. My second child can go to school. Who can argue with that?

A moustachioed officer, Nagare, also in epauletted khaki, appears.

Fish-Lips This is him?

Nagare This is the one they call Kalu.

Fish-Lips holds out clipboard and pen.

Fish-Lips Suspected tuberculosis, OK? Fill in the form. Tell the pathologist that's what we suspect. You won't have any problem.

He points at where Nagare is writing.

'Irrecoverable illness', that's what we call it. Then get him straight to the morgue.

Nagare Now?

Fish-Lips Super-now. Then straight to the crematorium. Get him off our hands.

Nagare is looking at the form.

Nagare Deepak Rai.

Fish-Lips I'm sorry?

Nagare That was his name. Known as Kalu.

Fish-Lips He was a street boy, that's all I know. 'Irrecoverable illness.' Get rid of him.

Nagare goes back to the stretcher.

Oh and don't tell the other boys, whatever you do. We
tell them it's murder.

Nagare Right. I'll take him away.

Fish-Lips Do that. Let's have a crackdown, shall we?

Nagare takes away the body.

1.11

*The police go. The Husain shack is now abutted by
another – with an entrance, a small, high brick-hole, a
door, a party wall. Annawadi's stage picture is beginning
to fill. A sewage pond, rubbish, trees. The characters are
beginning to inhabit their environment. From the second
house comes Fatima Shaikh, thirty-five, with one good
leg, a stump, a pair of metal crutches, too short so her
behind sticks out, gold eye-glitter and smeared orange
lipstick.*

Fatima A woman has rights. I have rights. From birth
nobody loved me. From the very beginning. Everyone
told me I was born wrong. And I believed them. I was
ashamed. I hated myself. Because I wasn't even a person.
I was an animal. One Leg, they called me. Why give a
thing a name? Why send a thing to school? People say
I'm a whore. How can I be a whore? Whores don't
choose. I choose. I'm in control. I choose who comes in
and I choose who doesn't. And if you don't like it, tough.
Fuck off. And if you do, remember, my husband's out
sorting garbage, my children are at school, drop by, I'm
in every afternoon.

1.12

Abdul and Mirchi appear carrying stuff from their adjoining house. Mirchi is younger than Abdul, just fourteen, cool, confident. There is now a huge pile of their stuff and of rubbish on the maidan. Karam is lying down. Fatima swings across on her crutches.

Fatima What's going on? What is this? What's this meant to be?

Mirchi We're rebuilding.

Fatima Starting when?

Karam Starting today.

Mirchi Before the monsoon.

Fatima Don't touch my wall. Whatever you do, I don't want it touched.

Mirchi Speak to our mother.

Fatima Zehrunisa!

Fatima has yelled. Zehrunisa appears at the doorway as if she's been expecting this. Abdul and Mirchi continue to go back and forth.

What's going on?

Zehrunisa What does it look like? Home improvement. We've decided to invest in our property.

Fatima What's the point? This whole place is going to be bulldozed.

Zehrunisa They've been saying that for years.

Fatima So?

Zehrunisa And it doesn't happen, does it?

Fatima shakes her head.

Fatima I know what you're up to. You want to show off. You want to prove you've got money.

Zehrunisa Actually, One Leg, can I tell you something? Rats eat our food because we have to leave it on the floor. Leave rice on the floor and the rats eat it. So believe it or not, we're tired of that.

Fatima You're tired, are you?

Zehrunisa What we want is a shelf. At a height we can actually work. So we don't have to squat. We want a new kitchen. See over there. See that. Karam is going out this afternoon to buy those very tiles. Beautiful Forever. That's what we're going to be.

She has pointed to the ad on the back wall.

Yes, we have the money, it's true. I don't deny it. And we're going to spend it. I don't see what's wrong with that.

Fatima You have to ask me. That's my wall.

Zehrunisa We don't have to ask you.

Fatima I'm not putting up with it. Last time you rebuilt, the noise was terrible.

Zehrunisa What, it disturbed your afternoon fucking?

Fatima What's it to you? What's it to you what I do?

Zehrunisa You should be ashamed of yourself. That string of disgusting men, hanging around your doorstep, drooling. Harassing my daughter.

Fatima Oh, jealous are you? What, because you can't attract a man? Except your wheezing dickless wonder of a husband.

She gestures at the prone Karam.

25

I'm not going to let you get away with this. It's not going to happen.

Zehrunisa It's going to happen.

Fatima goes in. After the tempest, it's suddenly quiet. Abdul looks, reproachful.

Abdul It's a mistake.

Zehrunisa Why?

Abdul To build.

Zehrunisa Why is that?

Abdul We're making ourselves a target. It's you who says people hate us. Now we're saying to everyone, 'Look how much money we have.' Why do that?

Zehrunisa Because we can.

Abdul Why throw ghee on an open flame?

Zehrunisa It doesn't make any difference. Whatever we do people call us shitty Muslims. Let's show we can live better than other people. So let's be shitty Muslims.

1.13

Darkness. The toilets: a yellow concrete block with red lettering. In her stall, Manju knocks on the ground, looking to contact Meena Chinnu, fifteen, a small, defiant Tamil, dark-skinned. She knocks back. An agreed signal.

Meena Manju.

Manju Did anyone see you?

Meena No.

Manju What's happening?

Meena The usual. I'm on lock-down. Tap and toilet only.

Manju Meena . . .

Meena I'm not allowed out. I get so angry.

Manju You mustn't. For your own sake.

Meena shakes her head.

Meena This morning, they started screaming because I was two hours at the tap. I said, it takes two hours.

Manju At least.

Meena It takes two hours! What can I do?

Manju waits, unable to answer.

I said again, I want to go back to school. My mother said, she won't let me. Ever. They're never going to let me, they say. I'm to prepare for my marriage, work in the home, nothing else.

Manju And then?

Meena I argued.

Manju And then?

Meena They beat me. They'll kill me if they ever find out I come here. And what we do when I get here.

Manju They'll never find out.

She looks at Meena a moment.

All right? Ready?

She takes a breath before leaping in.

There's this play called *The Way of the World*.

Meena *Of the World*?

Manju Yes.

Meena *Way of the World*.

Manju That's right. The men who are in it, they're called gallants.

Meena Gallants?

Manju Yes.

Meena Gallants. That's an English word?

Manju Yes.

Meena Is it used a lot?

Manju I don't know. This is the eighteenth century. That's three hundred years ago. There are people called Mirabell and Millament.

Meena Mirabell and Millament. Those are ridiculous names.

Manju I agree. And Mister Fainall . . .

Meena Fainall?

Manju Yes. He's the cuckold.

Meena A cuckold?

Manju A cuckold is someone whose wife is unfaithful.

Meena A cuckold?

Manju That's right.

Meena So here in Annawadi, you could say, like an example, you could say One Leg's husband.

Manju You could.

Meena He's a cuckold.

Manju He is.

Meena A cuckold! A cuckold!

She is over-excited.

Manju Shh!

Meena reins herself in.

A man called Congreve wrote it.

Meena Congreve?

Manju What he portrays is a very rigid society.

Meena Rigid?

Manju Yes. Everyone's in their own world. It's all about position and power. It's about doing well. And advancing.

Meena Advancing?

Manju Yes. In society. I'll tell you what they told me this morning. 'In Congreve's drama, money is more important than love.'

Both are momentarily silenced by this thought.

Meena Manju, do you understand it?

Manju What?

Meena The play?

Manju Don't worry, no one understands it.

Meena If you succeed, you'll be the first woman ever in Annawadi to get a college degree. You'll be an example to everyone.

Manju Meena . . .

Meena And I'll know nothing. I'll never know anything.

Manju You'll know a little. You know words in English.

She looks at Meena a moment.

Meena Manju, I'm never going to escape.

Manju Yes, you will. Don't despair.

Meena I have no life.

Manju But you will. If you learn.

Meena strains, thinking.

'Congreve's themes are love, social position and money.'

Meena Love, social position and money.

Manju Say it in English.

Meena does not speak.

Speak one word in English.

There are tears now in Meena's eyes.

Meena 'Love'.

1.14

The Airport Director speaks to us. He's in a smart suit and a hard hat.

Director Modernising an airport in Mumbai: it's like trying to do an open-heart surgery on a runner during a marathon. It's a problem. I don't pretend otherwise. This year in Mumbai we carry thirty million passengers. The plan is next year we carry forty. This is a city where everyone blames everyone else. We all complain about the poor, but, believe me, we're happy to employ them. At very low wages, because there are always more. This airport is still owned by the government but it's privately managed. We've made huge investments. Come on, if you make an investment, you expect a profit. Don't you? Isn't that what you expect? To do my job I need one thing. I need space. I need land.

1.15

At once the sound of hammering. For the first time, the whole slum is revealed – spatchcocked, lopsided shacks, some held together by duct-tape and rope. Slum lanes: mud, filth, litter, smoke, dirt, water, corrugated iron and, to the side, a sewage lake. The entire contents of the Husain house and their back room are out on the maidan. Fatima comes running out, in an outfit with pink flowers on it.

Fatima I can't stand it, do you know what's happening? Do you know what you've done?

Abdul appears from his doorway, desperate.

Abdul OK, OK, I know there's a problem, OK?

Fatima There's a problem all right. There's rubble in my fucking rice, my dinner is ruined.

Abdul All right, we saw this coming, just calm down.

Fatima I can't calm down. Why should I?

Abdul Calm down and listen.

Fatima I'm not going to listen.

Abdul Just listen, OK?

Zehrunisa appears at the doorway.

Zehrunisa What's going on?

Abdul Mother, please. Don't worry. I'll deal with this. Let me. Please. Mother.

Reluctantly Zehrunisa disappears inside.

Look, OK, there is a small problem, I admit, we do have a problem.

Fatima We have a fucking problem, all right.

Abdul We have a slab to make a new kitchen shelf.

Fatima is about to interrupt.

Just listen. What's happening is: I can't put it in. It won't stay up. It keeps falling down. So I need to make a hole in the wall.

Fatima You've made a fucking hole.

Abdul I know.

Fatima You've made it.

Abdul I know.

Fatima My house is falling down.

Abdul I'm going to put the shelf in the hole to secure it, then I'll cement it all over, it'll only take a few hours. It's because of the bricks. They're poor quality. They crumble. They can't take the weight.

Zehrunisa cannot resist coming out again.

Zehrunisa Abdul, just let me deal with her . . .

Fatima Ah, here comes cunt-face, couldn't resist!

Zehrunisa How dare you? How fucking dare you?

Fatima is waving her crutches dangerously. Abdul tries to intervene.

Abdul Both of you, please.

Fatima You've ruined my wall. Now you want to come out and gloat.

Zehrunisa It isn't your wall. You've never paid a fucking paisa.

Fatima What's that to do with it?

Zehrunisa Our family built it, remember. We paid for every brick.

Fatima Doesn't matter who paid. It's shared. It's a shared wall.

A neighbour, Cynthia, has appeared, alongside some others and is egging Fatima on.

Cynthia You tell them, Fatima. These Husains think they're so great. You think you're above the rest of us?

32

Abdul Keep out of it, Cynthia.

Fatima You're a fucking bitch. Up your hairy hole!

Cynthia That's right, you tell them, Fatima, time someone got hold of that cow.

Fatima Bitch! Fucking bitch!

Zehrunisa I may be a bitch but I'm not a slut!

At this, Fatima attacks her physically. There is now a crowd gathering to watch. Fatima is going to do Zehrunisa real harm, but Abdul interposes.

Abdul Mother, come on, what are you doing? What are you up to?

Zehrunisa She started it. Whore! Sister-fucker!

Cynthia has stepped in to comfort Fatima.

Cynthia Walk away, walk away, it's all her fault . . .

Abdul You're a mother of nine. You should be ashamed of yourself.

Zehrunisa She started it.

Abdul You should know by now. Just keep away from her.

Cynthia has put her arm round Fatima and led her indoors. Zehrunisa yells after her.

Zehrunisa While her children are at school! Sleeping with anyone who's even got half a dick.

Abdul All right, everyone, the party's over.

Zehrunisa What sort of mother does that?

There are ironic cries of 'Give us some more'. Fatima is coming back out on her crutches, followed by Cynthia.

Fatima I'm going, I'm going. Just you fucking wait. For what's going to happen. You have no idea. You're going to regret it.

The crowd cheers as she swings wildly off into the distance. Cynthia follows her.

Zehrunisa Where's she going?

Abdul It doesn't matter.

Cynthia You wait and see.

Abdul Come on, everyone, move on. Mirchi, all right? While she's away, let's get the work done, then at least it's over.

Mirchi Sure. Whatever you want.

Cynthia goes out and the crowd reluctantly disperse.

Abdul And Mother, you could do me a favour as well.

Zehrunisa Yes?

Abdul If we have a nice house, you know what I'd really like?

Zehrunisa What's that?

Abdul You could speak more nicely.

Zehrunisa I didn't start with the fucks. She did.

Abdul Even so. If we're trying to live nicely, let's live nicely.

Karam is returning from the same direction that Fatima went in. He's panicked.

Karam Someone tell me what that woman's up to.

Zehrunisa What are you doing here? I sent you out to buy tiles.

Karam I didn't have enough money. They're expensive.

Zehrunisa Oh fuck, how much more do you need?

But Karam is not answering.

Karam That doesn't matter. Listen, I just ran into some boys. They say Fatima's off to the police.

Abdul The police?

Karam She's putting in a formal complaint. She's accusing you of assault.

Kehkashan has appeared.

Abdul You need to run, you need to go after her.

Zehrunisa Are you crazy? I don't want to go near a police station.

Abdul You have to. You have no choice.

Karam Did you hit her?

Zehrunisa No, no, of course not. She's a cripple.

Abdul She's going to make up some stupid story. You need to catch up quickly and stop her.

Karam She's in a rickshaw.

Zehrunisa A rickshaw? But she hasn't got any money.

Karam She's got money for a rickshaw.

Zehrunisa Cynthia! Fucking Cynthia, I bet.

Abdul Come on, Mother, you can't wait any longer.

Karam Do I still get the tiles?

Zehrunisa How much are you short?

Karam Two hundred.

Cynthia has reappeared, laughing.

Cynthia I told you, she's going to fuck you over.

Zehrunisa Cynthia, was this your idea?

Cynthia What if it was?

Mirchi looks across with contempt.

Mirchi Fucking Christians!

Karam Do I still get the tiles?

Zehrunisa Yes. You get the tiles. You get the tiles! Whatever happens, we're going to have a nice house.

And she's gone.

1.16

Sahar police station. Papers, bureaucracy. A desk. A tall female officer called Kulkarni is listening to Fatima, who is crying profusely.

Kulkarni So what happened next?

Fatima She came charging towards me. She kicked away my crutches. You can see, I've only got one leg. I can't even stand. Then she beat me savagely.

Kulkarni Where? Where did she beat you?

Fatima All over. All over my body. It was a brutal assault. Merciless.

Zehrunisa appears, breathless from running.

Kulkarni And who are you?

Zehrunisa I'm Zehrunisa Husain.

Fatima It's her.

Zehrunisa Take no notice of whatever she tells you, officer. There were witnesses, they saw what happened.

Ask anyone who was there. Everyone'll tell you, Fatima Shaikh is a liar.

Fatima I'm not a liar.

Zehrunisa She's a fucking liar.

The two women have been yelling. Kulkarni loses patience.

Kulkarni All right, I've had enough. This is a domestic. You think anyone cares? We're here to guard an airport, there are terrorist threats. Drugs, guns. You think I give a damn about two neighbours who don't *like* each other? You, go home at once.

Fatima But officer . . .

Kulkarni I'm telling you. Now! Go home. Look after your children. Cook them dinner. Be a good mother. You're a stupid woman, get out of here.

Fatima It's not right.

Kulkarni It may not be right, but it's what's going to happen. You're a waste of time. Out!

Fatima This isn't the last! This isn't the last of it!

Furious, Fatima swings away and disappears. Kulkarni is looking at papers on her desk.

Zehrunisa Thank you, officer.

Kulkarni And where are you going?

Zehrunisa stops, looking across at her.

I want you to stay.

Zehrunisa Me?

Kulkarni Sit down over there. Sit.

Zehrunisa But I haven't done anything.

37

Kulkarni That's for me to decide. Sit down.

Zehrunisa sits on a bucket chair.

Zehrunisa I'm not a criminal.

Kulkarni heads out.

How long do I stay?

She's gone. Zehrunisa sits alone.

1.17

Zehrunisa stays sitting alone in the police station as Fatima swings home on her crutches. She moves down slum lanes at speed, grim, determined. She comes to her house. Next door, the Husains are working inside. Fatima goes into hers. From underneath her stove, she takes a metal can of kerosene. She puts it down in the middle of the room. Then she takes her jug of water, and pours some into a bowl.

1.18

At the police station, a contrasting silence. Then, smart, clean, Asha appears at the entrance.

Zehrunisa Asha.

Asha Tell me what's happening.

Zehrunisa Why?

Asha You know why. You're going to need my help. Who else can help?

Zehrunisa looks resentful, then concedes.

Zehrunisa All right. I'll tell you. They released Fatima but they asked me to wait.

Asha moves across to her.

Asha Zehrunisa, you know what they're doing. They know you've got money. They let Fatima go because she hasn't. You have no choice, You have to do business through me.

Zehrunisa No.

Asha I'm the go-to woman, I fix the police, I get the police to see reason. That's what I do every day. I'll get the family to withdraw the charges. Give me a thousand rupees and I can get the whole thing wrapped up in an hour.

Zehrunisa shakes her head. Asha gets up, quietly furious.

You people are mean, you know that? You bring your troubles on yourselves. What do they say of Muslims? Ten men pulling can't get your wallets out of your pockets. It's up to you. In this life, you make your own luck.

Asha goes. Zehrunisa is alone.

Zehrunisa Fuck. I've made a mistake.

At once Kulkarni returns with a cup of tea.

Kulkarni Here.

Zehrunisa What's this?

Kulkarni Tea.

Zehrunisa Is this for me?

Kulkarni And a biscuit.

Zehrunisa takes it. Kulkarni sits beside her.

You know what I'd do?

Zehrunisa No.

Kulkarni Beat the shit out of that cripple. Finish her off.

Do it properly. Why not? What's stopping you? If you don't deal with people like that, tell me about it, they make more trouble.

Zehrunisa speaks quietly, putting down a marker.

Zehrunisa I didn't hit her.

Kulkarni What I'm saying: if you decide to whack her once and for all, I'll look the other way.

Zehrunisa Thanks.

Kulkarni For a fee.

Zehrunisa hides her surprise at this turn of events.

You know you're behind in your payments?

Zehrunisa Yes.

Kulkarni Businesses aren't permitted on airport land. You're illegal. You haven't paid us for months.

Zehrunisa It was an oversight. I'm going to pay.

Kulkarni Well at least if you're here, you can settle. I'll find your regular officer.

Zehrunisa Thank you.

Kulkarni gets up to go out.

Officer.

Kulkarni Yes?

Zehrunisa This tea's very good.

1.19

The sound of Hindi film songs, turned up extra loud. Dusk in Annawadi, fires burning. The neon signs of the hotels beyond. Fatima has her door open, and can be seen swaying on crutches to the blasting music. She is

*painted extravagantly, like a Bollywood star, with red
lipstick and shining bindi. Kehkashan is sitting outside,
fuming, guarding the family possessions which are on the
maidan. Inside, Abdul and Karam are spading cement.
Fatima comes dancing out of her front door, and
Kehkashan gets up.*

Kehkashan I can't stand this. This is wrong. How dare she?

Abdul drops the spade and comes out, alarmed.

Abdul Kehkashan . . .

Kehkashan You know what she's doing? Our mother's
locked up, so she's celebrating.

Abdul Leave her. Honestly.

Kehkashan Why are they holding on to her? They let
Fatima go, and my mother's still there.

Abdul Come on, Kehkashan, it's you who always says
we shouldn't react.

Kehkashan You know what happens to a woman in a
police station at night.

*The crowd has begun to reassemble at the sound of the
music and Fatima's dancing. Kehkashan moves across
to her.*

Why hasn't my mother come home?

Fatima I haven't the slightest idea.

Kehkashan My mother's being held by the police and
you're dancing around like a film star.

Fatima Want some advice? You shut your face or I'll
have you arrested as well.

Kehkashan You see that leg? That leg there? The good
one?

Fatima What about it?

Kehkashan I'm going to twist it off, see how you like having no legs at all.

Cheers from the crowd.

Fatima You're going to pull it off?

Kehkashan Yes I am.

Fatima From what I've heard it doesn't seem likely. You and who else? A woman whose husband doesn't want to fuck her! He's never been up your cunt from what I've heard.

Karam is back from getting the tiles with Mirchi, and now goes nuts.

Karam Right, that's it, I've had enough of this, I can't take anymore. You insult my daughter. You accused my wife of beating you. I'll show you a beating. A proper beating.

Fatima Go on. What's stopping you?

Karam I'm going to.

Fatima Do it. Get on with it. I'm waiting. Here.

The crowd roar. He is too weak, so he turns to his son.

Karam Abdul.

Abdul What?

Karam You heard what I said. I'm giving you an order. I want you to beat her. Abdul! I'm telling you as your father. You must obey me.

Abdul stands a moment, agonised.

Fatima Come on, hit me. Come on, do it, why not? A defenceless woman with only one leg!

But Kehkashan has thought better of it and intervenes, putting her arm round his shoulder.

Kehkashan Father, it's not a good idea. Really. It's what she wants.

Karam Then give it to her.

Kehkashan It's a trap. I got carried away.

Karam She insulted you.

Kehkashan Yes. But she's trying to provoke us. That's what she wants.

Karam turns and shouts at Fatima.

Karam I'm going to charge you for half the bricks. Whatever happens, you're going to have to pay for your share of the wall.

Fatima Yeah. Well, you're going to need money, aren't you? For your own funeral. Because with what I'm about to do, I promise you right now it's not far off.

Applause at this. Fatima goes inside and slams the door. Everyone thinks the encounter has fizzled out and they disperse. Karam is being led back inside by his children.

Kehkashan Well done, Father, you did the right thing. It's over.

Karam All we have ever done is try and help her –

Abdul I know –

Karam For years –

Abdul I know –

Karam When her child died who looked after her? We did. We're Muslims together, we've done our best.

Abdul You're right. Let's get the work done and finished, the sooner the better. Then when Ma's back, we can all be friends.

Kehkashan has led her father inside. Meena is crossing the now-empty maidan and her mother Laxmi sees her.

Laxmi Meena, what are you up to? You're meant to be home. You're meant to be cooking dinner.

Meena I'm going home.

Laxmi You've been talking to boys.

Meena I don't talk to boys.

Laxmi If ever I catch you talking to boys –

Meena You won't catch me, because I don't do it. I don't. Why look at me like that? I don't talk to boys.

As Meena follows, she passes Noori, Fatima's eight-year-old daughter.

Hi, Noori.

Noori Hi, Meena.

Noori crosses to the door of Fatima's house. She tries to open it. She stands on a brick to see in the tiny hole at the top. Noori turns in panic, screaming.

Cynthia, Cynthia, where are you? Cynthia, help!

Noori has run across the maidan. Already Cynthia has appeared, and various other neighbours.

Come and help me, quick. It's my mother. I don't know what she's doing.

From inside, there is a whoosh and a boom. Cynthia runs across to the house. From next door, Karam, Kehkashan and Abdul are coming out at the sound of screaming. Cynthia and the neighbours batter down the door. From it emerges Fatima, on fire, the flames leaping, but her voice still strong as she points to the Husains.

Cynthia Here's a blanket, quick, roll her out on the floor . . .

Fatima This is what you've done, you did this to me.

Kehkashan Oh God, oh God help her.

The neighbours get her down on the floor, beating out the flames or smothering them with their own clothes. Asha comes running, Manju not far behind. Then Meena from another direction.

Asha What's happening? What's happening?

Cynthia She poured kerosene all over herself, then set light to it.

Asha Why on earth did she do that?

Cynthia She meant to burn herself a little, she burnt herself a lot.

Asha pushes through the crowd to where Fatima is now writhing on the ground. Kehkashan has moved Abdul away.

Fatima Water! I need water.

Cynthia She's still on fire, get water.

Meena I don't want to give her water. What if she dies? Her ghost will haunt me.

Cynthia Just get the water!

Meena goes to get it.

Manju Water's not good for burns. It's not. I promise. I read in a book.

Asha And if we don't, we'll have a dying woman's curse. You want that?

Manju No.

Asha Thanks. I'm not going to risk that. Give her the water.

Meena kneels to administer the water. The crowd falls back, and Fatima is visible. Her face is black and strips of flesh are hanging from her body.

Kehkashan Abdul, you have to get out of here.

Abdul What?

Kehkashan You know what the plan is. She's going to say it's our fault, that we drove her to it. She's going to say we set her on fire . . .

Abdul Why me? Why do I have to go into hiding?

Karam Because the whole family depends on you. The police'll be here in no time. If they take you, our family's finished. Do this for me, Abdul. We're ruined without you.

Fatima I'm hurting! Everything hurts!

Abdul, in agony, looks across indecisively to where Cynthia, Asha, Manju and Meena are all grouped round Fatima.

Cynthia Asha, you've got to get her to hospital.

Asha I'm not going to take her.

Cynthia It has to be you.

Asha hesitates, then hands money across.

Asha I'll give you the money for a rickshaw, here. You take her.

Fatima Somebody help me!

Asha Come on, Manju, we're leaving. Meena, you too.

Kehkashan Get going, Abdul, get out of here.

Cynthia Give her more water.

Abdul seems frozen. At the other side of the area Asha speaks quietly to her daughter. The sky has turned purple.

Asha I'm washing my hands of these garbage people. If Zehrunisa had coughed up when I offered to help, then none of this would have happened.

Fatima (*screams*) Help! Help! I'm in agony.

Noori (*crying*) Mother, Mother, Mother, we're with you.

Asha Small economies, big expense!

Cynthia Oh my God, her face is coming off. It's stuck to the ground.

Kehkashan yells at a traumatised Abdul.

Kehkashan Abdul! Run!

Abdul takes off at speed. Everyone else has gone. Noori is left alone with her mother.

1.20

At once the sound of an aeroplane approaching from the back. Everything shakes again, as the jumbo goes screaming over, lights flashing, apparently just yards above Annawadi. Then silence. Darkness. Just the sound of voices.

Sunil's Voice Are you there? Where are you?

Then the sound of pain.

Shit! Shit!

Abdul's Voice Sunil, is that you?

Sunil's Voice Yes.

Abdul's Voice Watch out for the rats.

Sunil's Voice Too late.

A streak of light. An eight-foot tangle of rubbish, all piled to the ceiling of the Husains' 120 square-foot garbage hut, next to their house.

Sunil Where are you?

Abdul I'm at the top. Be careful. One foot wrong and the whole lot goes down. How did you know I'd be in the store room?

Sunil I guessed. I wanted to see how you were.

He gets to the top. Abdul appears, squeezed down among the sacks.

Abdul, are you OK?

Abdul I've been awake all night. I could hear through the wall. The police came just after midnight. They took my father away. I heard them. They're accusing my sister too.

Sunil Your father's gone?

Abdul I felt such a coward.

Sunil You're not. You're not a coward. You need to get out of here before dawn.

Abdul If the police can't find me, they'll take it out on my father. They'll beat him even harder. You know how weak he is. I can't allow that.

Sunil Your mother needs you. The whole family needs you.

Abdul looks, not believing it.

48

Abdul No. I've made a decision. I'm going to give myself up.

Sunil Abdul . . .

Abdul It's guilty people who run. I'm not guilty.

Sunil Why on earth would you do that?

Abdul I think if I go in and tell the police the truth, at least my father'll be spared.

Sunil You think that's likely? You remember what happened to Kalu. You want that to happen to you? How can you trust the police? Every time we go out, they round us up. They beat us.

Abdul shakes his head.

Abdul I want to do it.

Sunil Why?

Abdul If I don't, then it's like saying I've something to hide. I've nothing to hide.

He gets up from the rubbish.

It's dawn. I'm going to go.

Sunil Abdul, don't do it. I beg you. It's you who always says 'avoid trouble'. One mistake, you say. Just one. It's you who says that. I'm telling you now: this is the one.

Abdul I'm going to go. I'm going to turn myself in.

He heads down the garbage pile. Not wanting to raise his voice, Sunil hisses at him.

Sunil Abdul! Abdul! Don't go.

But Abdul is already out of the shed. Dawn is breaking, Annawadi just beginning to stir. Abdul looks back, then decisively heads off and away.

49

I.2I

Burns Ward No. 10 at Cooper Hospital. It's cheerless, dirty. Fatima is on a bed, her face shiny black as if lacquered. She has a plastic tube in her nostrils, attached to nothing. An IV bag with a used syringe sticking out of it, and a rusty metal contraption over her torso, to keep the sheet from her skin. Her husband Abdul Shaikh, thirty-five, shovel-faced, is on a chair, when Poornima Paikrao comes in. She is in her thirties, with gold-rimmed glasses.

Paikrao Good morning. You're Abdul Shaikh?

Abdul Shaikh That's right.

Paikrao You're Fatima's husband?

Abdul Shaikh Correct.

Paikrao I need to speak to her. I'm a special executive officer. On behalf of the government.

Abdul Shaikh Ah.

Paikrao I need a witness statement.

Abdul Shaikh I thought she'd already done that.

Paikrao She has. But I need to update it.

Abdul Shaikh Why? Why do you need to update it? What are you saying? You didn't get it right the first time?

Paikrao looks at him thoughtfully.

Paikrao Perhaps it's better if you go outside while we do this. Please.

Abdul Shaikh goes and sits in the corridor.

Paikrao Fatima?

Fatima Yes.

Paikrao It's Poornima Paikrao. Special executive officer. If you remember, you gave me a statement.

Fatima Yes.

Paikrao In that statement you said three members of the Husain family poured kerosene over you, then threw a match and set fire to you. I'm not sure we're going to be able to maintain that account.

She waits but Fatima says nothing.

You see, since then I've spoken to your daughter . . .

Fatima To Noori?

Paikrao Yes.

Fatima You spoke to Noori?

Paikrao She looked in through a gap in the wall. She saw you pour the petrol on yourself. I'm afraid she's very firm about this.

Fatima begins to panic.

Fatima I want that family to pay.

Paikrao Yes.

Fatima I want revenge. Look at me . . .

Paikrao Yes.

Fatima This hospital has no medicine.

Paikrao I know.

Fatima The family must go to prison for this.

Paikrao stops. Even she is slightly awed by Fatima's determination.

Paikrao You see, if we just make a few changes. It's an offence under the old British law to incite anyone to suicide. It's a crime. So if that's what the Husains did . . .

Fatima They did.

Paikrao Good.

Fatima They made me do it.

Paikrao Clearly.

Paikrao has a statement on a clipboard.

You mentioned Kehkashan threatened to pull off your good leg . . .

Fatima Well, she did.

Paikrao Good. Then after that Karam said he was going to beat you . . .

Fatima He did.

Paikrao Then I think we can say, at his father's suggestion, Abdul attacked you . . .

Fatima Abdul?

Paikrao Yes.

Fatima Not Zehrunisa?

Paikrao No, not Zehrunisa.

Fatima I'd rather Zehrunisa.

Paikrao I know. But she has an alibi. And rather a good one. She was at the police station, remember? That might present difficulties. In the circumstances, I think we should just say Abdul.

Fatima OK.

Paikrao It was him that attacked you. Can you remember that?

Fatima Yes.

Paikrao He took you by the neck and throttled you.

Fatima Throttled?

Paikrao That's what I've written.

Fatima You've written it?

Paikrao Yes. I have it here.

Paikrao reads from the clipboard.

'As my left leg is handicapped, I could not retaliate. In anger, I put the kerosene lying in the house on myself, and set myself on fire.'

She smiles at Fatima, then starts to write.

All right?

Fatima You know I can't read.

Paikrao That doesn't matter.

Fatima I can't sign.

Paikrao produces an ink-pad.

Paikrao You can use your thumb.

Fatima holds out a burnt thumb as Paikrao reads out the words she has just written.

'Record made under clear light of tube-light.'

Paikrao presses Fatima's thumb to the pad, then puts it on the document.

Good. I can work with this.

Fatima People have come to see me. Since I came to hospital. I'm finally important. I'm an important person at last. At last I count. I count for something.

Abdul Shaikh comes back in.

Abdul Shaikh Excuse me, I'm hoping you can help us. My wife is really not well.

Paikrao No, well, that's not surprising is it?

Abdul Shaikh But she's getting worse. Nobody helps. The doctors don't come to see her. They say they don't want to touch her.

Fatima Something's wrong. I'm so cold.

Paikrao What have they told you?

Fatima Stay where I am.

Paikrao Anything else?

Fatima Drink three litres of water a day.

Paikrao Well, that's what you must do.

She looks at Fatima a moment.

At least you can relax now. Your case is safe in my hands.

1.22

Sahar police station. The back room. The sound of Abdul screaming. He is bent over a table, in handcuffs. Fish-Lips is standing over him with a leather strap in his hand.

Fish-Lips Why did you do it? Why did you do such a thing?

Abdul You have to tell me: what did I do?

Fish-Lips brings the strap down on him. Abdul screams.

Fish-Lips You beat her up.

Abdul Do you think I wouldn't have told you? I'm a coward, you know that. I would have told you. Please.

Fish-Lips hits him again. A howl of agony.

Fish-Lips You beat up a cripple. Why did you do that?

54

Abdul I didn't touch her. People were there, all around. Ask them, they saw what happened.

Fish-Lips I'm going to go on hitting you until you tell me.

Abdul I've nothing to tell you. Nothing!

The strap comes down a third time. Abdul is at his wits' end.

Why would I fight with a woman? I don't fight with anyone. Not even with my little brother. Ask. Ask my family. I've never hit anyone in my life.

Fish-Lips walks away a couple of paces.

Fish-Lips So tell me what happened.

Abdul Nothing happened. Fatima did it herself. She's jealous.

Fish-Lips Jealous of what?

Abdul Because we're richer than her.

Fish-Lips Richer, are you? I'd love to see some proof. Where's your mother? Why doesn't she come round? Share some of her wealth with me?

Abdul She will come. She promised she'll come.

Fish-Lips You know how ill Fatima is? She may well die. Then it's what we call a 302. You know what a 302 is?

Abdul Yes.

Fish-Lips If she dies, none of you'll ever get out.

He stands, thoughtful.

You're a sorter, aren't you, Abdul?

Abdul Yes.

Fish-Lips You need your hands. Show me.

Abdul holds out his hands.

They're small aren't they? Those cuts. Those stains. You think you're in a bad situation? You think your life has taken a bad turn? Not yet. Let's give your mother something to see.

Fish-Lips raises the belt and brings it down on Abdul's hands. Abdul screams.

1.23

Annawadi. Zehrunisa is sitting on the maidan when Poornima Paikrao appears, mild-mannered as ever.

Paikrao Ah good, yes, I'm glad I've found you. I needed a word.

Zehrunisa You'd better tell me who you are.

Paikrao You're Zehrunisa Husain. I'm the official in charge of your case. Or rather, should I say, your family's case?

Kehkashan appears silently from the house.

Paikrao This must be your daughter, Kehkashan. She's not in jail?

Zehrunisa No, she isn't.

Paikrao For the moment.

Zehrunisa and Kehkashan wait.

I take all the statements, that's my job.

Zehrunisa Really?

Paikrao Effectively it's my decision whether this case ever reaches court or not.

Zehrunisa Are you saying you can stop it?

Paikrao Well, that's up to you, isn't it? One thing I could do, and this would finish the whole business at a stroke, I could go and see Fatima's husband for you. I could put an end to it. Well?

Zehrunisa looks, judging how to play this.

Zehrunisa I've already been.

Paikrao You've been? You've been to see her husband?

Zehrunisa Yes. I made him an offer.

Paikrao What sort of offer?

Zehrunisa I offered to move Fatima to a private hospital. Pay for everything – her bed, her medicine, her food.

Paikrao You were wise. You know what they say about Cooper Hospital? When you go to Cooper, you go *upar*.

She points upwards.

And did her husband accept the offer?

Zehrunisa Not yet. He's thinking it over.

Paikrao You want my advice?

Zehrunisa I can see I'm going to get it.

Paikrao You should hire a professional. A professional negotiator. That's one of the other things I do. If you give me fifty thousand, in cash, then I shall hand it to him. Most of it. I can do that for you. And everybody's stories will match.

Zehrunisa is wracked, uncertain. Paikrao is sweet and calm.

Zehrunisa I need to think. It's a difficult time.

Paikrao Oh, it's certainly that all right.

Zehrunisa Whatever happens: I want to do the right thing.

Paikrao smiles.

Paikrao Ah yes. The right thing is always difficult. But funny how people always find it eventually.

1.24

Abdul is thrown violently by a couple of police officers into an informal holding cell, lined with filing cabinets and desks. He is battered and bruised. There are six or seven prisoners, all shackled, including Karam. Father and son lie together on the tiles.

Karam Abdul, it's you.

Abdul Father.

Abdul is holding his hands between his legs.

Karam Your hands! Show me your hands! Abdul, what have they done? What have they done to you? Let me see.

Obediently he holds out his battered, bruised hands.

Oh my God, Abdul, oh my God! How can you work? How will we live?

1.25

Sahar police station. Fish-Lips is at the desk as Zehrunisa comes in.

Fish-Lips Yes?

Zehrunisa I've come to visit my husband. Karam Husain. And my son.

Fish-Lips They've been charged.

Zehrunisa Charged? Can you tell me what they've been charged with?

Fish-Lips Yes, I can.

He has taken out a clipboard and is holding it up.
Zehrunisa gets the idea and tentatively reaches into her
pocket. She pushes some rupees across the desk. He
just looks. She pushes some more.

Are you taking the piss?

Zehrunisa No.

Fish-Lips Do you think we're stupid? You treat us like
idiots? The Husains are rich. Everyone knows that. You
think you're better than everyone else? You think the
rules don't apply? Seeing the charge sheet will cost you
five thousand.

Zehrunisa starts to panic.

Zehrunisa I don't have that kind of money with me. I'm
going to go home. Please don't – please don't do anything
to them while I'm away. I'll be back in no time at all.
Please, I'll be grateful, if you show mercy. Sir, I'll be very
grateful. Will you wait? Can you wait? I'll take that as a
yes.

Zehrunisa runs off. Fish-Lips just watches, then
answers the phone.

1.26

The door of the police station opens and Fish-Lips looks
down at Abdul and Karam.

Fish-Lips Time to get going.

Abdul What's happened?

Fish-Lips I warned you. It's a 302. It's murder. You're
being moved.

The maidan. The two shacks, side by side. The slum-dwellers have begun to gather, Manju and Meena among them. Manju holds out her hand.

Manju The first spots of rain.

Meena The monsoon's coming.

Manju Not yet.

Meena Soon.

There is silence, as other women arrive.

Manju Just the first spots.

Kehkashan comes out of Fatima's doorway.

What's happening?

Kehkashan We're washing the body inside.

Zehrunisa comes out, upset, heading for her own house. Kehkashan looks at her.

Well? Do we have to do it? Do we?

Zehrunisa We have to.

Almost blinded by tears, she goes inside her house. The women wait. Then Zehrunisa reappears with a cotton quilt with tiny blue checks.

Kehkashan It's our best quilt.

Zehrunisa It's our only quilt. The body's not wrapped. It has to be wrapped.

Kehkashan I love that quilt.

Zehrunisa I have to. I have no choice. One Leg gets our quilt.

Zehrunisa disappears inside Fatima's house.

Kehkashan looks at the other women a moment, then follows her in. Asha appears.

Asha Ah, there you are.

Manju Yes.

Asha What are you doing?

Manju We're waiting.

Zehrunisa reappears, a rag in her hand.

Zehrunisa We've washed the body. We've washed her sins away. Now let's get the men.

The women come out of the house as Manju makes a move.

Manju I'll get Mr Kamble.

Asha No.

Manju Why not? He'll want to be here. He knew Fatima well.

Asha Mr Kamble died.

Manju He died?

Asha Yes. Two days ago.

Manju He died and you didn't tell me?

Asha says nothing.

What happened?

Asha Happened?

Manju Yes.

Asha Nothing happened. What did you expect? He had a bad heart.

Everyone turns as four men move into the house. They include Mirchi and Abdul Shaikh. People continue to gather, while at the other side of the stage two Doctors, one male, one female, in white coats appear with papers.

1.28

First Doctor Fatima Shaikh?

Second Doctor Yes.

The Second Doctor reads from a clipboard.

'Greenish yellow sloughs formation all over burn injuries with foul smell. Brain congested, lungs congested, heart pale.'

First Doctor She came in with thirty-five burns six days ago. It doesn't look good. Change it to ninety-five burns on arrival.

The Second Doctor writes. The First Doctor nods, satisfied.

Change it to ninety-five and file it away.

1.29

The Doctors go. From the house, a white metal box is carried out, the bier secured by poles, held by the four men. The people stand as it goes by. Zehrunisa is holding Kehkashan's hand as it passes. When it is gone, Zehrunisa puts a few possessions in her hand and embraces her.

Zehrunisa Now you must go.

Kehkashan nods.

Asha You'll be all right.

Kehkashan I'll see you soon.

Kehkashan leaves.

Manju Where is she going?

Asha She's joining her father and brother in jail.

The slum-dwellers disperse. Asha, Manju, Meena and Zehrunisa are left standing alone, stunned.

Zehrunisa The rain'll come soon.

The four men carry the bier on poles down the road, the men not varying their step. It is carried off. The monsoon begins, flooding the area. Everyone runs for cover in the pelting rain.

End of Act One.

Act Two

2.1

It's raining at a bus stop. Zehrunisa is in full burqa. She speaks to us.

Zehrunisa I've made mistakes. I know that. I've made mistakes from the start. You're looking for the right person. They're out there somewhere. Waiting to be bribed. Money! Money, yes, of course, money of course, but in whose hand? I spend the whole day visiting relatives. I tell them, I've sold our back room. They look at me, pitiless. I know what they're thinking. 'You should have paid the first bribe. On the first day. The very first one. If you'd paid the first bribe none of this would have happened.'

2.2

Annawadi is a monsoon flood bowl, the brimming sewage lake at the centre, with nothing but the BEHIND THE BEAUTIFUL FOREVER *wall and the hotels beyond. Fish-Lips is approaching through the rain, obviously angry. Zehrunisa turns at once.*

Zehrunisa Officer, I'm sorry . . .

Fish-Lips What the hell happened?

Zehrunisa I can explain. Forgive me.

Zehrunisa falls to her knees.

Fish-Lips Where the fuck have you been? We had an arrangement, remember?

Zehrunisa Of course I remember. I'm very grateful, officer.

Fish-Lips It's up to you. If Abdul isn't a juvenile, then he's in trouble. If he's an adult, he goes to Arthur Road

Jail. If you want to say goodbye to your son, or if you want him to come out a cripple. It happens.

Fish-Lips shakes his head.

To me, he looks like a grown-up.

Zehrunisa I really don't think he is. He's worked his whole life. He never went to school.

Fish-Lips You really don't know how old he is?

Zehrunisa I do remember one thing about his birth. It was about the time Saddam Hussein was killing people. I remember Saddam Hussein was doing bad things.

Fish-Lips Well that narrows it down. That really helps.

He is sarcastic, but Zehrunisa protests.

Zehrunisa I stopped in the road. He was born outside the Inter-Continental Hotel. He didn't look like a baby. I looked down, he was in a pile of dirt, he looked like a rat.

For the first time Fish-Lips softens.

Fish-Lips That's a nice hotel.

Zehrunisa It is.

There is a brief moment of contact.

Fish-Lips I'll tell you what I'm going to do for you.

Zehrunisa Thank you.

Fish-Lips I'm going to find you a school certificate. Do you know what that is? Saying he attended this school or that. Saying which class he was in.

Zehrunisa How old are you going to make him?

Fish-Lips I was thinking sixteen. Shall we? Sixteen seems right.

Zehrunisa It may even be true.

She takes money from inside her garment. Still on the ground, she hands notes over to Fish-Lips.

Fish-Lips He can avoid prison. He can go to the Youth Detention Centre.

Zehrunisa How's that?

Fish-Lips Dongri isn't too bad. Considering.

Zehrunisa He'll be pleased. For the first time in his life, Abdul'll know his age.

2.3

Dawn. The sound of the amplified call to prayer from mosques outside. Allah u Akbar: God is Great. Dongri Youth Detention Centre. The shell of a colonial sandstone structure painted pink. Pictures of Gandhi, Nehru and Ambedkar. A different India. An enormous flat floor, on which 120 boys sleep laid out in a barracks in rows. The Guards arrive, a whistle blows.

Guard All right, everyone, time to get up. Get to it. Let's get going. Come on.

The Guards patrol, handing out rags, as the boys get to their feet and go to wash at a line of upstage taps. At the front, Abdul has sat up and is rubbing his eyes, not moving. A pockmarked Guard comes by.

Guard Husain, are you going to wash? Are you refusing to wash?

Abdul does not react.

If you don't wash, you don't get breakfast.

Abdul I don't wash every day.

Guard Why not?

Abdul Because there's no point. I work in rubbish. I just get dirty again.

66

The Guard waits. Abdul says nothing.

Guard What is it? Some kind of protest?

Abdul No.

Guard We don't have protests.

*Another Guard calls out, 'All right everyone here.'
Abdul gets up. His uniform is too large, trousers
puddling at his feet. His hands have filthy bandages.
They stand in a circle and, with surprising enthusiasm,
sing the National Anthem. Then they all sit down in
the circle to be given breakfast – rice and hard bread.
The Guard points at Abdul.*

This one gets nothing.

*The Guard goes. Abdul sits alone while everyone else
eats. The boy next to Abdul speaks to him.*

First Boy You're being stupid. It's the first rule.

Abdul What is?

First Boy In Dongri. Don't do anything stupid. Why
aren't you washing? Everyone washes.

Abdul And what's the second?

First Boy What?

Abdul If there's more than one rule?

First Boy The second is that you're guilty.

Abdul Guilty?

One or two of the boys laugh.

First Boy Yeah. Whatever you did. Doesn't matter. Just
say you did it. It's easier. It's just much easier. 'Did you do
it?' 'I did.' '*I did.*'

*He has raised his voice in mock-terror, and now all the
boys join in.*

First Boy 'Did you steal that saucepan?'

All I did. I did.

First Boy 'Did you steal that radio?'

All We did. We did.

First Boy 'Did you steal that bicycle?' 'Did you kill your father?' 'Did you strangle your mother?' 'Did you rape your sister?'

All Guilty. Guilty.

There are improvised interrogations from all over: 'Did you kill twenty people?', 'Did you poison your uncle?', 'Did you sell ganja?', with everyone laughing: 'Yes I'm guilty, I did it, I confess, I confess.'

First Boy You see, there you are. If anyone asks you, just own up.

Abdul Why?

First Boy Because, it's obvious, that's what they want. Give them what they want! Why not?

The pockmarked Guard has reappeared.

Guard All right, everyone, this morning you have a teacher.

There is a collective groan.

No, really, every day you're meant to have a class. Well, today for once you do.

Second Boy Who is he?

Guard He's called the Master. Face this way.

The Guard makes lines with his arms to denote where they are to sit, all facing one way.

All right, sit and wait here. He's coming.

The Guard goes out.

First Boy I don't believe it. What a fucking waste of time.

The Master comes in. He is middle-aged, pudgy, with high-rise hair and watery pink eyes. He reaches the point of command, then speaks into a microphone.

Master Good morning, everyone.

A Few Good morning.

Master It's a pleasure to be here. It's a privilege to have the chance to speak to you at such a moment in your lives. When you're all facing challenges. Let me say one thing before I say anything else: I have faced those challenges also. We're made from the same clay, you and I. The extraordinary thing is, I've seen so many boys come through this place, and I shan't lie to you. If you were my boys I would have thrown you all away long ago.

The boys laugh.

Because I can see your destiny, that's why. It's as if I'm looking at a map, and it's already drawn, because I know for a fact how few of you are going to come through. There's only one way to survive in life. The boys who take the path of honour live. The boys who take the path of crime die. That's how it is.

There is a silence among the boys.

It's the most extraordinary coincidence. I'll tell you. Because if you live dishonestly, you're going to die young. Your families disown you, they stop visiting you, you spend most of your life in prison, and then one day, when you're thirty or thirty-five, you die on the pavement. And that's what I call a coincidence, because doing the right thing, living well, living honestly doesn't just make you feel better but – hey, think about this! – it's actually in

69

your own interest. All you have to do is choose. You choose. And you. And you.

He has pointed to three boys at random, including Abdul. The Master is beginning to choke up.

Yes, I can see one or two of you are beginning to cry, and I don't blame you – because I'm crying too. Matter of fact, I've done a lot of crying lately because I've just been through a very painful divorce. I was married to a woman who wasn't very nice. My God, what a bitch. And that's a hard thing to face up to when you love someone. She was such a bitch she took my car in the divorce settlement. But I let her take it. I gave away a Ford Fiesta. I said, go on, if you want it, take it.

Tears are pouring down the Master's face as he is moved by his own story. Abdul is still, transfixed.

OK. And that's what I'm saying. Because – believe it or not – not long after, I got a new girlfriend. And this girlfriend – now I'm crying again because I'm thinking about her – but you should meet my girlfriend. You really should. She's a much nicer person than my wife ever was. And also, by the way, she's much better looking. So there we are. I did the right thing and I got my reward. Because you see, I'll tell you the interesting thing, being good is the right way to live.

The Master looks round.

Thank you, everyone. Be sure to use well the rest of the day.

The Master moves away. As the boys disperse, Abdul moves to catch him.

Abdul Excuse me, sir, I wonder if we could speak.

Master Of course. What do you want to say?

Abdul hesitates, unused to this.

Abdul Everything you say makes sense. I'd never heard it before.

Master I wouldn't say it if it wasn't true.

Abdul I don't think I've lived a bad life, sir. But I never went to school. I never learnt. I never had time to think.

The Master looks at him.

I like this place. It gives me a chance to think.

Master Tell me your name.

Abdul Abdul Husain.

Master Abdul, it's good to meet you. I meet many boys. If I can help one then I'm not wasting my time.

Abdul I'm in here because I'm accused of a crime. But I didn't do it.

There is just a flicker in the Master's response.

Master I have other appointments. I'd love to talk longer, but I can't. If you need to get hold of me, Abdul, ask the authorities. I'll be very interested to hear what happens to you.

The Master goes out. The boys have dispersed. Abdul stands alone, wondering.

2.4

Annawadi. Asha's place is relatively well appointed, with a television set. Manju and Rahul are readying it for a family party.

Manju All right, over here, lay them out, potato chips and chocolates . . .

Rahul Look, napkins!

Manju Put the chocolates here.

Rahul You put these under the chips.

Manju Why do you put napkins under chips?

Rahul Don't ask me, but that's what you do.

He demonstrates with paper napkins.

It's me who's worked in a hotel.

Manju You only worked there a week.

Rahul Eight days. At the Inter-Continental. Magic!

Manju You were sacked.

Rahul I wasn't sacked. I was let go. They'll take me back.

Manju They told me you danced with the guests.

Rahul I didn't dance with the guests. I danced for the guests. It's different.

Manju How is it different?

Rahul There was music, 'Rise Up', you know? And it's a pretty belting song, some people were drunk, they said 'Show us some Mumbai moves.'

Rahul does some moves and sings:

Rise up, don't falling down again'
Rise up, love like I broke the chains!

The head waiter came up. 'Have you gone mad, asshole?' I said. 'You told me always to give guests what they wanted. They wanted me to dance.'

Manju You're an idiot.

Rahul laughs at the memory, as Asha appears. She's in a dark blue sari, looking splendid.

Asha Well, I must say it's beginning to look beautiful.

Rahul Thank you.

Asha You're both doing a marvellous job. Let's just hope this isn't the last birthday I have here.

She has sat down to work on her make-up.

Mahadeo Why should it be?

Manju In Annawadi? Why?

Asha Because – can you believe it? – they've started talking again about knocking us down.

Manju I don't believe it.

Mahadeo They're always talking about knocking us down.

Asha Again!

Mahadeo It's just talk.

Asha Make way for the airport!

Manju It's not going to happen.

Asha It's going to happen one day. There are bulldozers out on Airport Road.

Manju Come on, there are always bulldozers on Airport Road. What do your sources say? If anyone knows what's going on, you do.

Manju grins at the others at this.

Asha I'll tell you exactly what they say –

But then Asha's mobile goes off.

Rahul I want to hear this. Does she know something? Are we all going to be turned into a car park?

Asha (*on phone*) Hello. Hello. No. No, I'm sorry. It's my birthday.

Mahadeo Who is it?

Asha (*on phone*) My children have laid on a party. No, I don't think I can. Really. Another day. Call me.

She quickly clicks it off.

Well there you are, you see, the work never stops.

Mahadeo Is it work?

Asha That's the bore of being the go-to woman. They expect you to help them every hour of the day.

Manju is looking to Mahadeo, who is obviously suspicious. She has a knife for the cake in her hand.

Manju Mother, turn it off. You're never going to be forty again. Rahul and I have worked all day to prepare the party.

The phone goes again. Asha scrambles for it. Manju raises her voice.

We did this for you!

Asha (*on phone*) Yes? No, I've said. Really I can't. I can't. I won't change my mind. Call me back in five minutes.

She turns the phone off, goes to the mirror and starts fluffing her hair.

Manju I don't believe it. I don't believe this is happening.

Asha What's wrong? I'm just doing my job.

Manju That's not the tone you use when people come to you in trouble.

Mahadeo Manju . . .

Manju You were being positively pleasant. Who was it? Where are you going?

Asha I'm not going anywhere.

Manju Then why are you standing in front of the mirror?

Asha is betraying her nervousness by the clouds of talc filling the air. Mahadeo is formal.

Mahadeo Asha, in the name of our marriage, I have to ask you . . .

Asha Please don't ask me anything.

Mahadeo I have to demand that you –

Rahul What's going on?

Mahadeo You have to stay. We're a family! You know how much this party means to us all.

The phone goes again. Each syllable comes out crisp, rhythmic, as her family stands round in silence.

Asha (*on phone*) Yes. Yes. Yes. Yes, see you then. Can't wait.

She clicks it off.

I have to go out.

Manju No.

Asha I have to. I promised. It's as simple as that.

Manju Where are you going?

Asha It's none of your business.

Mahadeo Asha, I'm your husband. Where are you off to?

Asha I'm not taking any shit. I'm not. I keep this family together, that's what I do. Who else can do it? And I'll do it in my own way. When I need to. And don't anyone ever tell me otherwise. I won't be late, I'm not going to be late.

Sweating, Asha makes to go out in a cloud of talc.

Mahadeo Asha, I'm begging you. Don't go.

Manju reaches out for Asha's hand as she passes. But Asha breaks free of her grasp and goes out. Mahadeo has tears in his eyes. No one can move.

No one say anything. No one's to speak. No one's to speak of this. No one.

Manju looks to the floor, knife still in hand. Rahul is stunned, disbelieving.

2.5

The other Mumbai pours on to the stage. Outside the entrance to bright pink Grand Maratha Hotel, a brightly dressed wedding party, behind a fence, passes with a loud brass band playing, confetti flying. Paparazzi. Asha appears and stands a few moments, fascinated, in the ambient light. Then the wedding party go inside. The band disappears. All at once, it's dark and windy. An Officer appears at the other side, fifties, heavily built, smoking a cigarette.

Officer I'm glad you could make it. We need to be quick.

Asha No problem.

She crosses to him. He stubs out his cigarette.

Officer I've only got fifteen minutes. The car's round the back.

The Officer puts his arm round her. At this moment Zehrunisa appears on her way to the prison. The two women see one another for a moment. Then Asha and the Officer leave.

2.6

The women's prison. A line of female prisoners, among them Kehkashan, waiting for visitors. Zehrunisa arrives, apologetic, harassed.

Zehrunisa I'm sorry. I'm sorry, I tried to be on time.

Kehkashan Have you brought me anything?

Zehrunisa I brought you chocolates.

Kehkashan Is that all you got?

Zehrunisa hands across one bar.

Zehrunisa Have they given you a date –

Kehkashan Not a word.

Zehrunisa For your trial? Have they told you?

Kehkashan They tell us nothing.

There is a moment's silence.

You don't look well.

Zehrunisa The world has changed since you were in prison. Times are difficult everywhere.

Kehkashan We were doing so well.

Zehrunisa I felt like a navigator, steering a boat. I was proud. 'You're a very good navigator,' I would say to myself. Then the storm blows up, and sends you off course. All that skill goes for nothing. Makes no difference what sort of sailor you are.

She shakes her head.

I'm running around town asking for money. All our relatives. All our friends. They don't care. To them, we're just entertainment, we're a story. We're something you talk about when you're bored.

A bell goes off. End of session. Others begin to get up.

Kehkashan You'll come back tomorrow?

Zehrunisa nods.

How's my father?

Zehrunisa He still has faith. He says in court he'll get justice. He believes in the system.

Kehkashan If we ever get there.

Zehrunisa Prison isn't good for his lungs. If I don't get money he'll die.

There is a moment.

Kehkashan And Abdul?

Zehrunisa Abdul's fine. That boy can look after himself.

2.7

Darkness. The toilets again. Manju discernible first, then Meena.

Manju Meena?

Meena Yes.

Manju So you're there.

Meena Of course I'm here.

Manju You didn't come yesterday. I thought you wanted to learn.

Meena appears beside her.

Meena Manju, I think all the time about Fatima.

Manju Why?

Meena What she did.

Manju Why do you think about her?

Meena Because her ghost is here in the toilets.

Manju I don't think so.

Meena I've heard it. Most of the women won't come inside. They'd rather shit round the back. I hear Fatima screaming and cursing. I hear her ghost.

Manju just looks at her.

I wouldn't burn myself. That's not how I'd do it.

Manju Meena.

Meena I'd never set fire to myself because then you leave people with a bad memory. Do it so you look good at the end.

There's a silence.

Manju Meena, why are we talking about this?

Meena Don't say you haven't considered it.

Manju I don't want to discuss it.

Meena Why not? You say the flowers in my hair never turn sticky and brown. That's because I never bottle bad things up inside me. Flowers die in your hair because you never dare to speak out what you feel.

Manju hesitates.

Manju Everyone's thought about suicide. It's human.

Meena When?

Manju Just a few weeks ago.

Meena What happened?

Manju It was to do with my mother.

Meena It's always your mother.

Manju No, but this was different. I discovered something about her. She's doing certain things. For my sake. For my education. I felt dishonoured. I felt there was only one path to take.

Meena But you didn't take it.

Manju No. I thought about it but I decided it was wrong.

Meena Wrong? And is it right to live when you have no hope?

Manju You have hope.

Meena My family allow me nothing. I'm fifteen years old and they're sending me to marry a man I don't know, in a village I don't know, hours and hours from here. I'm to live my whole life knowing nothing, thinking nothing, because they won't allow me to learn. That's my story, I've left nothing out.

Manju It doesn't have to be.

Meena Yes it does. I'm going to have a life but I'm not going to live.

She gets up, decisive.

And that's what Fatima felt.

Manju Nonsense.

Meena Trapped. I understand her.

Manju You're wrong. It was an accident. Her friend Cynthia told her to do it. Cynthia said, 'Set fire to yourself.' Fatima made a mess of it.

Meena shakes her head.

Meena I wouldn't make a mess. I'd take poison. It's clean.

Manju Don't be ridiculous. You couldn't even look at Fatima, remember. The sight of her made you ill for a week.

Meena That's because she did it wrong.

Manju You have to stop saying such things.

Meena What's the point of our meeting if I can't say what I think? You're the only person I can speak to at all.

Unusually, she has raised her voice. Manju can't answer.

I met a boy.

Manju Meena . . .

Meena My brother brought a friend home from work. A city boy.

Manju Well?

Meena Then he began to phone. I had to tell him, 'If they see me on a phone, I'm dead.'

She shakes her head.

My life's unbearable.

Manju It's only just begun. You have to let it play out.

Meena Why?

Manju Because killing yourself is like giving up. It's like saying you're beaten.

Meena But, Manju, I am. I am beaten.

She makes to go.

I have to go. No, really . . .

Manju Meena . . .

Meena You're a good friend to me, Manju.

She looks at Manju.

Manju, you've been a good friend.

2.8

Annawadi. Sunil, alone, speaks directly to us.

Sunil Something happened in America. Something bad. There's a street called Wall Street. Everyone says 'Wall

Street'. They all say 'Wall Street's crashed'. I asked the man who runs the games parlour. He knows everything. He said, 'The banks in America went in a loss, then the big people went in a loss. A lot of Americans are living in their cars or in tents under bridges.' And here I can tell you what's changed. A kilo of empty water bottles – a few weeks ago, you got twenty-five rupees. Today you get ten. A kilo of newspaper was always five rupees. Today they give you two. And it happened suddenly. We'd stopped eating rats. Some years ago. 'In Annawadi, we don't cook rats,' we said. Now we cook them again. One day, a world we knew. We could live. Next, Wall Street's down and no one's making a living. Anywhere.

2.9

At once a plane goes over, low, deafening, shadowy. Sunil has been joined by Taufeeq, across a distance in the empty space. Taufeeq is older, darker, in trendy clothes.

Sunil Taufeeq.

Taufeeq German silver.

Sunil No.

Taufeeq German silver.

Sunil Taufeeq, you know I can't.

Taufeeq It's there. We both know it. It's waiting.

Sunil looks at him mistrustfully.

Sunil Do you know the price? The price has fallen.

Taufeeq Everything's fallen. Everything. German silver's fallen less than everything else.

Sunil How much can you get?

Taufeeq I can get sixty a kilo.

Sunil Sixty? It used to be a hundred.

Taufeeq The world's changed. Sixty's not nothing. And we know where it is.

He waits, tempting Sunil.

Taj Catering Services.

Sunil No.

Taufeeq Why not?

Sunil It reminds me of Kalu.

Taufeeq So? And you? Are you even eating? How tall are you, Sunil? How tall? Will you ever grow?

Sunil moves away, hurt. Taufeeq knows he's prevailing now.

Sunil Why do you need me?

Taufeeq Why do you think? I've seen you. Climbing up coconut trees. Like a monkey. You're fast. And you judge risk better than anyone.

Sunil No.

Taufeeq moves in, decisive.

Taufeeq We've both seen that gap in the fence. Behind a bush. At the end of an unlit lane. Let's be serious, it's like an invitation.

He waits, but Sunil says nothing.

Sunil, how big is Mumbai?

Sunil Big.

Taufeeq How big?

Sunil Very big.

Taufeeq And how many people live there? Taj Catering Services has a gap in its wire. What are the chances, if we don't go in, someone else will?

Sunil High.

Taufeeq How high?

Sunil reluctantly smiles, for the first time.

How high?

Sunil As high as the stars.

Taufeeq nods, his point proved.

I always said I wasn't a thief.

Taufeeq All right, that's fine. We agree. You're not a thief.

Sunil Good.

They both smile.

Taufeeq You're not a thief who happens to be stealing some metal tonight.

2.10

Dongri. The gates outside the great Victorian building. Abdul, back in his own clothes, with a small parcel under his arm, stops at the gate where the pockmarked Guard holds out a clipboard for him. His hands are still bandaged.

Guard Here. Sign here.

Abdul takes the pen from him and signs.

Sign here again.

Abdul does a second signature.

And now you're out. You have to report back every Wednesday.

Abdul Officer, I've been thinking about your job.

Guard I beg your pardon?

Abdul It isn't easy, is it? Looking after so many boys. So

84

much responsibility. I've realised how hard it is. I've been looking at it from your point of view.

The Guard stares at him.

Guard Just fuck off, will you?

Abdul Yes, sir. Thank you.

He walks, his bundle under his arm, and as he does, the whole of Mumbai, in all its confusion and vitality goes by. Abdul walks, thinking.

2.11

Annawadi. The rain has stopped, and it's drying out. All the rubbish is laid out in front of the house. Where once there was bounty, now it's pitiful. Mirchi sneaks back, trying not to be seen. But Zehrunisa, in burqa, is out of the house, quick as a flash.

Zehrunisa Where the hell have you been? Where have you been to?

Mirchi I was out to get a job.

Zehrunisa This rubbish needs sorting. Look at it. The whole family depends on you, Mirchi.

Mirchi has sat down in the rubbish and started picking at it in a desultory way. Zehrunisa is furious.

Mirchi I met a man. He says he can give me a job in a car park counting cars. I'd be good at it.

Zehrunisa You're crazy. Nobody owes you a living. This town is full of people cleverer than you.

Mirchi It's at Sky Gourmet. The wages are good there.

Zehrunisa You worked there before. You lasted three days.

Mirchi It was good money.

Zehrunisa Yes but they never paid you.

Mirchi It was still good money!

Zehrunisa Yes, if you'd got any, it would have been good.

Abdul appears. They are both taken aback.

Abdul What's happening?

Zehrunisa Abdul. You're back.

Abdul Yes. They agreed to release me on condition I go to report every week.

Zehrunisa I can't believe you're here.

Abdul Where's all the stuff? Is this all we have? I come back and there's nothing left?

He stands, suddenly dominating.

What about the store room, is that empty too?

Zehrunisa I sold the store room.

Abdul You sold it?

Zehrunisa I'm always out trying to get money.

Abdul I was gone six weeks, not six years.

Zehrunisa And Mirchi's been running the business.

Mirchi I'm no good at it. It's not my thing.

Abdul Tell me about it.

Mirchi shrugs, all charm.

Have we lost all our pickers?

Zehrunisa Not all. Most.

Mirchi I'm sorry, Abdul.

Abdul stands looking round, hands on hips.

But also, don't forget, there's a global recession.

Abdul A what?

Mirchi There's something called a global recession. It began in Wall Street. A black man's going to run America.

Abdul What's that to do with it?

Mirchi I'm just saying. Same name as us. Barack Husain. I thought you'd be interested.

Abdul I'm not interested.

He is despairingly looking through the stuff.

Zehrunisa Abdul, I'm asking. I need to ask you to come back to work. The old team. Me the brain, you the hands.

Abdul shrugs, the whole answer.

Abdul I've never refused you. Only this time, I have to warn you, I made a decision, it's going to be different.

Zehrunisa Different? How?

Abdul I want to stop buying stolen goods.

Zehrunisa looks, wary, warning.

Zehrunisa Abdul, you have to be careful. I don't think you know how tough it is right now.

Abdul I've heard.

Zehrunisa For everyone.

Abdul I've heard.

Zehrunisa The world doesn't work in our favour. Six weeks ago, remember, we were going to expand. Now we're fighting to survive. We're the same people.

Abdul doesn't react. Zehrunisa loses it.

I don't even know what it means. What the fuck does it mean? Not buy stolen goods? What are you going to do?

87

Ask? Every time someone comes to sell. 'Where did you get it?' Are you crazy? Everything's stolen. One time or another. If not from this person, at least from the person before. You think anything's *pure*? I don't think so. It's all shit. We deal in shit, that's what we do. And you're going to start saying 'Where did this shit *come from*?'

Abdul In Dongri, every night I thought about it. What it would be like to be honest. And if it means we lose out, if it means we make less money, then we live with that. That's the price we pay.

> *There is a new steeliness in Abdul. He undoes the bandages from his hands, and casts them silently aside. Then he sits and starts once more to sort garbage. Zehrunisa looks at him mistrustfully.*

So? Do you agree?

2.12

Navratri Festival. The decorations have gone up, there is a flagpole on the maidan as Manju walks across to look for Meena, who is trying to dance with everyone else, but who is reeling around unsteadily.

Manju What's wrong? What's happened?

Meena Nothing's happened.

Manju Tell me what happened.

Meena Nothing.

> *She looks at Manju a moment. She's quiet.*

I rang the boy.

Manju You didn't.

Meena My mother heard. She beat me. Then my brother wanted me to cook him an omelette for lunch, while I was fasting. He beat me. I'm going to be sick.

Manju What is this? I don't understand.

Meena has turned aside to spit.

Open your mouth.

Meena No.

Manju Let me smell your breath. Meena, let me smell your breath.

Meena opens her mouth. Manju smells.

How much did you take?

Meena doesn't answer. Manju runs across to Laxmi.

Laxmi! Laxmi! She's taken rat poison.

Laxmi Is that what she's saying?

Manju She's not just saying it. Look.

She holds out the empty tube.

Laxmi I don't think so. She pretended to do that before.

Manju This time she's done it.

Laxmi I know what she's up to. Because she's angry with us. Navratri's got to her. She wants some pity. Well she's getting no pity from me.

She turns round and goes back inside.

Manju We need to find tobacco. We have to find something to make you sick.

Meena Manju, you don't understand. I don't want to be sick. I've done it carefully. Just like I promised, remember? I took it with milk. I've done it before. And it never stays down. It always comes up. This time it's going to stay down.

Manju No. I'm going to get salted water.

Meena It's not what I want. I blame no one. This is what I wanted.

Manju Well you can't have it, Meena, d'you hear?

She stands, shaken to her roots, her whole being engaged now. The Navratri Festival returns, loud music.

You can't have it. You may want it, but you're not getting it.

She runs off wildly, shouting for help.

Help! Please! Anyone! Salt water! Help!

Meena begins to convulse as, oblivious, the Navratri dancers sweep back on to the maidan. The whole population goes by, hands joined, as Meena lies on the ground, her guts twisting her in agony.

2.13

Navratri continues. A noodle-wali is selling chicken chilli and rice from a mobile stall. Sunil is eating from a paper plate, when Abdul appears, going home.

Sunil It's you.

Abdul Yes.

Sunil Hey.

Abdul I haven't seen you. Where have you been?

Sunil Oh, you know. Hanging about.

Abdul nods, an awkwardness between them.

How was prison?

Abdul And you? What's that? You've got something in your ear. You always wanted an earring.

Sunil I did. It's a skull.

Sunil fingers the metal ring, self-conscious.

Abdul You're different. Sunil, have you grown taller?

Sunil Two inches.

Abdul Well done. You always wanted to be taller. Even more than an earring.

Sunil Both. I wanted both.

Abdul's about to set off.

Come and I'll buy you a meal.

Abdul I can't.

Sunil Why won't you? Chicken chilli and rice.

Abdul shakes his head.

Abdul. I've had some good luck.

Abdul Yes, I can see that. The earring.

Sunil hesitates, then jumps in.

Sunil All right, I can tell you what happened. We've found this amazing gap in a fence. It's wild. So far I've picked up twenty-four pieces of iron.

Abdul Well done.

Sunil I take them out in my trousers. It's like taking cake from a child.

Abdul Good. Then you're all right.

Sunil Abdul. What's wrong? What happened in jail? I know you. You're changed. Say. Fucking say.

He suddenly shouts.

I had nothing, Abdul. I was eating the grass in the lake. For fuck's sake have some chicken chilli and rice. Have it. Do me a favour, I want to buy you a meal!

He sounds so agonised, Abdul cannot refuse.

Abdul All right.

Sunil Good, let me get it, man. When did you last eat?

Abdul Yesterday morning.

Sunil Shit. There you are. Well that's what I'm saying.

He has sped across to the woman on the stall.

Another chicken chilli and rice. A big one.

He turns back to Abdul.

Fuck. You're so fucking difficult, man.

Abdul I think I'm easy.

Sunil I can tell you you're not. (*To the woman.*) Yeah,
extra rice, please. And more sauce. As much as'll fit on
the plate. Here.

*He holds out money. The woman takes it. Sunil carries
the piled, steaming plate across to Abdul. He hands it
over in silence.*

Abdul Thanks.

Sunil Now will you tell me what's going on?

Abdul has finally let go of his cart. He shrugs.

Abdul I've been thinking. One morning I was lying on the
floor. In the prison. All the other boys. Sleeping. I could
hear them breathing. And I thought: we're all the same.

Sunil All the same?

Abdul People.

Sunil People are the same, is that what you're saying?

Abdul No, I'm saying something more interesting than
that. I'm saying we're all made from the same stuff. But

92

we can make ourselves different. Like, for instance, water. It can be dirty water. Just water. Nothing else. Or it can be ice. Everything's made of the same. But it can be better than what it's made of.

He stops and looks straight at Sunil.

Sunil, I want to be ice.

He waits. He becomes embarrassed.

I'm not used to eating so much. Don't get me wrong, it was great. But it's too much.

He holds the plate out, making to leave.

Sunil What's going on, man? You don't want to be friends? You don't want to be friends with me? What, I'm not good enough?

Abdul looks down at his plate.

Abdul Can I take it with me?

He turns and goes. Sunil stands alone.

2.14

The car park at night. Sunil and Taufeeq scale the side of the half-finished building with astonishing agility, German silver in hand. Taufeeq hangs from the side, speaking in an urgent whisper, as Sunil goes higher.

Taufeeq What the hell are you up to? Sunil, where are you going? We need to get out of here.

Sunil I'm going up to the roof.

Taufeeq What for? There's nothing on the roof.

Sunil I'm going up. You get going. See you later, OK?

Taufeeq The guards are coming back. What are you doing, you stupid arsehole? You're going to get caught.

He is alarmed. But Sunil is on his way.

Sunil I need to go on the roof.

Taufeeq climbs down as fast as possible and disappears. Sunil climbs on to the roof. When he gets there he looks out across Mumbai. From the street below comes the sound of Om Shanti Om. *Sunil starts to dance, sketching in at first, and then with more abandon.*

2.15

Asha's place. Asha runs in – triumphant, transformed. Manju is teaching a six-year-old.

Asha My darling, oh my darling daughter.

Manju What on earth's happened?

She gets up, bewildered.

Asha And you could say, it's all down to you.

Manju To me?

Asha Well, only partly. I had the right kind of charity, but you, my darling, you have the right job.

Manju The right job for what?

Asha I've been talking to a man called Bhimrao Gaikwad.

Manju I've never heard of him.

Asha At the Maharashtra Education Department.

She cannot contain herself.

In twelve months we could be out of this place.

Manju Out of Annawadi?

Her children are smiling at Asha's euphoria.

94

Asha There's a government programme. To give everyone in India an education.

Manju Everyone?

Asha Exactly. Regardless. Child labourers, disabled, girls.

Manju But that's great.

Asha You and I are going to run twenty-four kindergartens.

Manju How on earth are we going to do that?

Asha has got out a piece of paper and is holding it up.

Asha Gaikwad's given me the names of the teachers.

Manju The names of the teachers? He gave you their names?

Asha He said, use these.

Manju Use them?

Asha He said, these are the ones you have to put on salary. We write their cheques, we take them round.

Manju Hold on, Mother, are these people real? Are they real teachers?

She sends the child away.

The whole thing's a scam? Is that what you're saying? You're saying the schools won't actually exist?

Asha They'll exist on paper.

Manju So who gets the money?

Asha We do. Government money! It's the best kind.

Manju moves away.

Manju No, I'm not doing this. This time I'm not going to do it. I won't. I want nothing to do with it.

Asha Manju, how do you imagine you've got as far as you have? I do what I do, so you don't have to. Corruption gets a bad press, but for us it's our best hope. And it's not our corruption. It's theirs. They thought of this scheme. Not us.

Manju turns, suddenly furious.

Manju I nearly killed myself! Do you know that? I thought about killing myself. I talked to Meena about it. Before she tried. This man Gaikwad, I know what you're doing. I know how you got into this scheme. Everything we have is because of – what you do at night. You shame us, Mother. You shame us by your behaviour.

Asha How else do you think people get on? They use what they have. That's what everyone does. One thing I've learned from first-class people: if you don't think it's wrong, then it isn't. Us, we wait a whole lifetime for one opportunity like this. But for them, these things fall in their laps all the time. I believed in competition. Truly. Getting the advantage. Getting ahead. And I was good at it. And after all these years, I live by a sewage lake with a drunken husband. Take the chance you're given and be grateful. If we don't do it, then tell me one thing. Tell me how else we progress.

Laxmi appears like a ghost at the door.

Laxmi Well, I hope you're happy.

Manju What? What's happened?

Laxmi You've got what you want.

Manju moves away, shaken.

My daughter was in the hospital. She died this morning.

Manju She was getting better. Every day she was meant to get better.

Asha moves forward, directly opposite Laxmi.

Asha I'm very sorry, Laxmi. I'm shocked.

Laxmi My daughter took poison, and then later she died. Now where do you think she got that idea?

She turns and looks at Manju. Asha, shaken, looks between them.

Asha I don't know what you're saying.

Laxmi Don't you? Turns out for the last year, she never told us, but these girls have been meeting. Did you know?

She waits.

Did you know?

Asha I sort of knew.

Laxmi Did you or didn't you?

Asha I didn't think there was any harm in it.

Laxmi They met in the toilets. In the toilets. Why do you think they did that?

Manju turns, desperate.

Manju Mother, this isn't fair. Tell her this isn't right.

Asha I must say, as far as I understand it, Manju was trying to educate Meena.

Laxmi Educate her? Educate her to what?

Asha Broaden her mind.

Laxmi Is Meena's mind broad enough now?

Manju is horrified.

Manju It isn't my fault. I tried to stop her, it was me that tried to dissuade her.

Laxmi Did you?

Manju I was worried about her.

Laxmi You were worried, were you? So did you come to the family? Did you come and tell us?

Manju looks desperately to Asha for help.

Manju You beat her. The whole family beats her.

Laxmi We beat her to make her obedient.

Manju No. To make her submit. That's why you wouldn't educate her. So she wouldn't have thoughts of her own.

Laxmi just looks at her.

Laxmi You took our daughter, you told her about novels, and men, and the ways of the world. We want nothing to do with you. You call it education. I don't. I call it rebellion. You killed our daughter.

Manju It's not true. Mother, tell her it's not true.

Laxmi turns and goes out. Manju throws herself into Asha's arms. Asha accepts her, hugging her.

I did nothing wrong.

Asha I believe you.

There is the sound of a ring-tone. Manju is hysterical.

Manju Don't take it.

Asha It's my phone.

She lets Manju go and takes out her phone. The sound of an approaching plane. Lights, noise, the shadow goes over.

2.16

Sunil turns on the top of the building, the plane passing right over his head. He begins to climb down. He moves quickly into the darkness. Out of nowhere two Security Guards appear. One grabs him by the neck, the other starts to rip off his clothes.

First Guard Do you think we're stupid? Do you think we don't see you up there?

Sunil I'll give you money. Here, take everything I have. Take it.

He has reached into his pocket, coins tumbling out.

First Guard Hold him! Hold him! Take off his clothes.

Sunil Please, I promise, I can get you much more.

He is stripped to his underpants. One Guard takes the aluminium pieces he has in there and throws them to the ground. The Second Guard has got a cut-throat razor which he opens and brandishes in front of Sunil.

Second Guard I don't think you'll ever go thieving again.

They push him down on the ground. They hold him by his hair. The Second Guard raises the knife. Sunil screams.

2.17

P. M. Chauhan steps forward to address us. She is in her forties, in black robes, with bright red lipstick. The wire fence goes and is replaced by her Sewri courtroom.

Chauhan It's very hard to live on a judge's salary. Don't let anyone tell you otherwise. People think we're well paid and we're not. And the pension arrangements aren't simple. Sometimes I think I'll wait for the next pay hike and then get out. Have you heard of fast-track courts? Cases were taking eight, ten years to be heard, so Delhi decided there should be fourteen hundred new courts all over India. I run one. I have – let me think – thirty-five cases, maybe thirty-six, and each day I hear evidence from eight or nine of them. You need a good memory. You listen to poor people all day, fighting among themselves. She said this, he said that. They don't seem

99

to realise. It suits everyone fine. Perfect. Couldn't be better. Let them fight among each other. That way they're not fighting us.

2.18

Chauhan goes into her courtroom in Sewri. It's more like an encampment – empty plastic bottles and cans in front of the high judge's platform. There are nine or ten different prisoners, some of them shackled. Kehkashan, now in burqa, and Karam share the prisoners' bench. There are rows of brown bucket chairs. It's full of families and the public, and two tiers of metal desks with Prosecutors, Clerks, Defenders.

Chauhan All right, let's get this thing going, please, we don't have all day. I've an awful lot to do.

She starts shuffling papers and turns to her Clerk as the public flood in.

We are on the burning case, is that right? Those wretched women.

Clerk That's what we're doing.

Chauhan Next witness. Cynthia Ali. Is Cynthia Ali here?

Cynthia I'm here.

Cynthia puts up her hand. She has dressed in a spectacular purple sari. She rushes forward as Abdul Shaikh, thrown by the speed of it all, is led away.

Chauhan We already have a written statement. Go to it, please.

The Defender has the statement and is already starting.

Defender You're Cynthia Ali?

Cynthia I am.

Defender And you say in the statement you were Fatima's best friend?

Cynthia I was a good friend to her.

Defender And now you're working – what? – in the anti-poverty business?

Cynthia I'm a social worker.

Defender Yes, but you didn't use to be, did you?

Cynthia No. I've just started.

Defender That's right. First of all you were an exotic dancer. Then you moved into the garbage business, is that right?

Cynthia My family, yes, we sorted rubbish.

Defender And that collapsed last year? And would it be true to say the Husains had taken most of your custom by then?

Cynthia A lot of it, yes. That was luck.

Defender Luck?

Cynthia Zehrunisa has a son who's the best sorter in the business. It isn't fair. That's not fair competition. He was so fast it was unnatural.

She is defiant. A few people laugh.

Defender Their business prospered, yours failed?

Cynthia says nothing.

Where were you when Fatima set fire to herself?

Cynthia I was at home.

Defender And what were you doing at home?

Cynthia I was chopping vegetables. Noori called for me, I went straight across.

Defender So you arrived at the scene only after she'd already lit the petrol. That's right, isn't it?

Cynthia Yes, but I saw what happened.

Defender What exactly did you see?

Cynthia I saw the Husains, all three of them, attacking her, hitting her with a stone.

Defender You saw from your house, did you, while you were chopping vegetables?

The Defender smiles, content.

Where is your house?

Cynthia I'm her neighbour.

Defender Yes, but your house is in a different slum lane altogether.

Cynthia It's not far.

Defender It isn't anywhere near, certainly not in sight of Fatima. You never saw any so-called vicious fight, did you? In fact, you're lying, aren't you?

Cynthia I'm not lying.

Defender You were in a house with no direct view. And now you're lying about it.

Cynthia I'm not lying. I'm not.

Chauhan is looking at her watch.

Chauhan Ah good, excellent, that point's established. The witness admits she's lying.

Cynthia I don't admit I'm lying.

Chauhan The witness says she saw the fight, but she didn't. Thank you. We get the message.

Cynthia is outraged.

Cynthia I haven't finished.

Chauhan No, but we have. Come on, let's get the husband up.

Cynthia This is crazy! This isn't fair!

Clerk If the husband's quick. Then you can break the back of the whole case today.

Then she sees that the Prosecutor is already guiding a confused Abdul Shaikh to the stand.

Chauhan Very good, sir, well done, up you go. The quicker the better. That's why it's called a high-speed court. You get the idea. OK, take the oath.

Abdul Shaikh takes the oath. The oath isn't finished, but Chauhan has turned.

OK, are we ready? Come on, let's go.

The Prosecutor, eager to please, is already on his feet. Abdul Shaikh is looking bewildered.

Prosecutor Your name's Abdul Shaikh?

Abdul Shaikh Yes, sir.

Prosecutor And what relation were you to Fatima Shaikh?

Abdul Shaikh I'm her husband, sir.

Prosecutor And when she set fire to herself, you weren't actually there?

Abdul Shaikh No, sir. I was at work. I took her to the hospital.

Prosecutor And on the way to Cooper Hospital, what did she say?

Abdul Shaikh looks nervously to Chauhan, who seems impatient.

Abdul Shaikh She said that Kehkashan, Karam and Abdul had all insulted her.

Prosecutor And did she say anything else?

Abdul Shaikh prepares himself. Then:

Abdul Shaikh She said the three of them held her down by the neck.

Prosecutor By the neck?

Abdul Shaikh Yes, sir.

Prosecutor And what did they do then?

Abdul Shaikh They beat her, sir. With a stone.

Prosecutor They beat her with a stone?

Abdul Shaikh Yes, sir.

Prosecutor All three of them?

Abdul Shaikh Yes, sir.

Prosecutor Good, that's very clear.

The Prosecutor sits but the Defender is already up. He has floppy hair and a pin-stripe suit.

Defender I think I'm right in saying that your wife had recently been very depressed.

Abdul Shaikh No, sir. That isn't correct.

Defender You lost a child? Your daughter? Your wife lost her daughter and she wasn't depressed?

The Defender smiles at the unlikeliness.

There's a history of this, isn't there?

Abdul Shaikh History?

Defender Suicide attempts. This isn't the first time she set fire to herself, is it?

Abdul Shaikh This was the first time, sir. The neighbours drove her to it. That's why she did it. Because they attacked her.

Defender She said they attacked her. That's what she claimed. How do you know she wasn't lying?

Abdul Shaikh My wife was never a liar. She did many bad things. She did. But why would she lie?

Karam shouts out.

Karam She lied all the time.

Abdul Shaikh Why would she lie?

Karam She lied. She lied.

Abdul Shaikh Why would she lie when she knew she was dying? It doesn't make sense.

Karam My whole family's in prison because of her lies.

They are shouting over each other.

Chauhan All right, that's enough. One more word and you're in contempt of court, sir.

Zehrunisa (*standing up*) He's only trying to tell you the truth.

Chauhan One more word and you go to jail as well. We're going to take lunch. I've heard enough, I've heard enough of this. We'll resume this case in eight weeks.

The Judge goes. Zehrunisa rushes over to try and speak to Karam, who is being led away.

2.19

Asha comes out of her house, gleaming with a new confidence. As she does, Zehrunisa appears at the other side, in burqa. The two women are alone on the empty stage. They look at each other warily.

Asha I tried to help you. I told you. I knew what lay ahead for you. I've seen it so many times. At least your son's out of prison.

Zehrunisa He is.

Asha Until he goes back.

Zehrunisa He won't go back. He's out. He's staying out.

Asha Is he?

She thinks a moment.

Do you have any money left?

Zehrunisa Why should I tell you?

Asha Do you have anything?

Zehrunisa shakes her head. Asha has sounded sympathetic and for a moment it seems as if she might help. But then her manner hardens again.

You'll need to sell your house. I can find you a buyer.

Zehrunisa I'm sure you can.

Asha Think about it. I'll get you a good price.

Zehrunisa I'm sure you will.

Asha For a commission. I'm here for you. I'm always trying to help.

Zehrunisa smiles, then begins to laugh. She goes.

2.20

Abdul is sitting working at a pathetically small pile of rubbish. Poornima Paikrao arrives. Abdul looks up.

Abdul And so what is it this time?

Paikrao Well, that's a fine way to greet me. I want to speak to your mother.

Abdul You can't. She's exhausted. The trial has upset her.

Paikrao I'm bringing her news.

Abdul What sort of news?

Paikrao She's not going to like it.

Abdul Mother!

Zehrunisa comes out from the house.

Paikrao They're changing the judge.

Zehrunisa Mirchi!

Abdul When?

Paikrao They've done it already. Judge Chauhan's moved to another part of the state.

Mirchi appears from inside.

Listen, I know this is bad news, but I think I may be able to help you.

Zehrunisa It doesn't make sense.

Paikrao I can imagine. This must be shattering for you.

Zehrunisa The judge had heard all the evidence. How's the new judge to understand what happened?

Paikrao He'll work from a transcript. That's what I'm saying. I have to tell you, this new judge has quite a reputation.

Abdul looks up, alert.

Abdul A reputation for what?

Paikrao Let's just say, he's not known to be a merciful man. Everyone says he likes to hand out long sentences.

Abdul Long sentences?

Paikrao Yes.

Abdul That's an extraordinary coincidence.

Paikrao Why?

Abdul Because the last judge, remember, you told us she handed out long sentences too.

Paikrao shuffles a little.

Perhaps you've forgotten. Interesting, isn't it?

Paikrao But that's exactly why I wanted to speak to you. With this one, I've been able to go directly to the clerk of the court. I think there's a real chance I can get the trial abandoned.

Abdul Abandoned?

Paikrao Yes.

Abdul You think you can get the whole trial stopped?

He has got up with a strange and uncharacteristic determination, taking Paikrao on.

And would that be the present trial or would that be mine as well?

Paikrao Well, I think, to be fair, one thing at a time. Deal with yours later.

Abdul And can you give us some rough idea of what this might cost?

Paikrao Cost?

Abdul Yes.

Paikrao Well, obviously, there are going to be a number of people who are going to need to be compensated.

Abdul Obviously.

Paikrao The clerk. Some police officers.

Abdul Yourself.

Paikrao I think we're looking at two hundred thousand.

Zehrunisa slumps. Without warning, Abdul suddenly yells out to a couple of passing slum-dwellers.

Abdul Everyone! Please come and join us. There's an official here from the government with a fascinating proposal. Let me introduce you all to Poornima Paikrao. She works for the government.

Paikrao What are you doing?

Abdul She's saying Father's trial can be stopped for a mere two lakh.

Zehrunisa Abdul, what are you up to?

Abdul Me? I'm not up to anything.

Zehrunisa Are you mad?

Abdul No, Mother, I'm asking everyone to look at her. She's someone who must think we're idiots. Because what she doesn't tell us, she doesn't actually have the authority to stop the trial. It's not in her power. Even I know: it's a criminal trial. What do you think we are? Stupid ignorant people who don't know any better?

Neighbours are gathering round.

Paikrao Don't raise your voice, people are listening.

Abdul Two hundred thousand rupees! That's two hundred, everyone.

Paikrao is shaking her head.

Paikrao All right, play this game, but I warn you, if you don't pay, then things are going to get much, much worse.

Abdul I actually don't see how things could be worse than they are! Do you?

He stands, hands on hips.

Look at us. You're like dogs. Licking at us, taking what's left of our blood. You've already taken our lives. All right, so we let you do it. But there's a limit. And my mother's reached it. Do you understand? She's paid the police, the people in the prison, in the courts, the neighbours, anyone who held out their hand. And tell you what? This is a great day. Because this is the day we stop. We stop.

Zehrunisa smiles, proud of him.

Zehrunisa Abdul, you're a fucking good boy.

Paikrao You're going to regret this.

Abdul Hey, I got a better idea. We're going to pay you in rubbish. Why not? That's what we trade in. That's our stuff. Here. Have a bottle.

He starts throwing rubbish at Paikrao, just the odd thing at first, then his rhythm becoming fanatical, till he is pelting her.

How many bottles d'you need? We got bottles. Take 'em. We're going to pay you in plastic, is that all right? Take it. Take it. Why not take it? Here it is. Have it. It's yours.

At this moment the bulldozers arrive, and with a great crash the wall at the back begins to shake. It crumbles, then the bricks shatter, and the machines behind are revealed. The slum-dwellers all come running out. 'It's happening, it really is happening, it's happening at last.' Out on to the maidan comes everyone: staring in astonishment, the warring families side by side. 'It's begun, it's just at the edges, it's not the whole village, it's just the wall, they're only doing the wall.'

Zehrunisa Here it is, at last, they said they'd do it, and now here they are.

Everyone turns as the bulldozer takes another mammoth bash. The whole wall now falls to the ground. The bulldozer goes back. Paikrao turns and leaves.

2.21

The new judge, C. K. Dhiran, comes weaving through, and, as he does, the sewage lake is filled in, the walls removed, and the village disappears. Dhiran is bony, his sleepy eyes behind gold-rimmed glasses. He heads towards his podium in the court to be greeted by the Clerk of the Court.

Dhiran Ah, good morning, good morning. I read one last night we can do very quickly. Do we have the Husains?

Clerk Yes. They're here.

Dhiran Let's get them in and put them in front of me.

The Clerk calls out as people now pour into the courtroom.

Clerk Quiet, please, everyone, now we're starting. Silence! Everyone quiet. Calling Karam Husain! Kehkashan Husain!

Kehkashan and Karam come pushing through the crowd. Zehrunisa and Abdul are also present.

Karam Here, Your Honour. Present!

Clerk Please, the two of you, up on the stand.

Father and daughter head for the witness stand. Dhiran smiles at the two of them from behind his glasses. Kehkashan is in her burqa.

Dhiran Good morning. So you must be Kehkashan Husain, is that right?

Kehkashan Yes, sir.

Dhiran And what do you do?

Kehkashan I do housework.

Dhiran Well, I hope it's you, Kehkashan. It could be anyone hiding under that thing.

Dhiran laughs modestly at his own joke. The Clerk smiles. Dhiran turns to Karam, whose lungs are so bad he can barely speak.

And you, sir, I take it you're her father?

Karam I'm Karam Husain, sir.

Dhiran Yes. And what do you do?

Karam Sir, I work in plastics.

Dhiran Plastics? I suppose that means plastic bottles and bags. You collect them, yes? Why not say so?

Again, Dhiran seems amused.

Now you're accused, as I see it, of driving your next-door neighbour to suicide by repeatedly beating her up. So what shall I do? What's the best thing for me to give you? Two years? Three?

He has a big smile on his face. Suddenly he lifts both his arms above his head.

Ridiculous. This case should never have been brought.

Karam Sir.

The Prosecutor gets up.

Dhiran Sit down. I don't see how it's even got this far. Unless somebody was making money out of it. Come on, this was an everyday quarrel that got out of hand. I can't find anything more sinister than that.

Karam Sir.

Dhiran Both of you, get out of here as quick as you can.

Karam Now?

Dhiran Yes, now. Right away. You're not guilty. Either of you. Get out of here.

Karam Yes, sir. At once, thank you, sir.

Kehkashan Thank you very much, sir.

Dhiran Don't thank me, you did nothing wrong.

Karam Can I just say thank you, sir?

Dhiran Now, please, let's move on to the next one.

Zehrunisa has begun to cry.

Clerk Next case up, please, aggravated murder, assault, robbery! The accused to step forward, please.

They are backing off the stand, Karam still saying 'Thank you'. Abdul Shaikh starts shouting.

Abdul Shaikh This is wrong. This isn't right. What happens to me? I've lost my wife! We've lost everything! What do we get? We get nothing!

Noori is trying to comfort him. But no one else is taking any notice. Kehkashan has fallen into her mother's arms as everyone leaves the court.

Karam I always told you. Didn't I say from the start? In an Indian court, a man can get justice. Isn't that what I always said?

Zehrunisa Yes, it is.

But then she sees Abdul Shaikh standing by with Noori, defeated. She touches Karam's arm and silently nods in Abdul Shaikh's direction. Karam looks at him a moment, and then walks over.

Karam Abdul Shaikh.

Abdul Shaikh Yes?

Karam Are you going back to Annawadi?

Abdul Shaikh (*shrugs*) Where else can I go?

Karam Please. May we all walk to the bus together?

Abdul Shaikh looks at him, reluctant. Then, tearful, he nods. Zehrunisa and Kehkashan fall in beside the two men and the child. The five of them walk together towards the bus stop. They stand, forming a queue. None of them speaks. They wait.

2.22

Zehrunisa shows us her wrist.

Zehrunisa I wear this thread. It's a red thread. I went to Reay Road, there's a mystic there. What she does, four things: improving futures, relieving tensions, removing curses, appeasing ghosts. I went for all four. She told me the spirits will be friendlier now. I will always wear this thread. It's to ward off Fatima's ghost.

2.23

Zehrunisa goes. The Mithi river, at dawn. A road over a bridge. Under the bridge, there is a ledge, covered in litter, and two massive outlet pipes below. Sunil appears, looking terrible, exhausted, holding a bag of rubbish. His head has been shaved. He leans over, looking down to the ledge. Abdul comes by, pushing a three-wheeled motorised cycle which is perilously loaded with rubbish to a point where it might tip over.

Sunil Hey, it's you, man.

Abdul Yeah. What happened to you?

Sunil Oh.

Abdul You look like hell.

Sunil I know.

He grins.

Sorry to ask, but you don't happen to have two rupees, do you?

Abdul I've got two rupees, yes.

Sunil To give to me?

Sunil has come beside him. Abdul reels back.

Abdul Oh Sunil, do you have any idea what you smell like?

Sunil That's one of the things about people, isn't it? They can't smell themselves.

Abdul Then you're a very lucky man.

Sunil The fart has no nose.

Abdul What's a thief doing out at dawn?

Sunil smiles. The old charm.

Sunil Look at you. Suddenly you're in transport.

Abdul I can't make a living picking rubbish, I can't make a living sorting rubbish, so now I try and make a living moving rubbish.

Sunil How's business?

Abdul How do you think?

Abdul looks at him a moment.

Often when I'm riding this thing, when I'm in traffic, three cars that side, four the other, I think, 'One mistake, just one mistake, one wrong turn and, hey – I don't exist.'

Sunil Hmm. I quite like that feeling.

Abdul So do I.

Sunil Yeah.

Abdul I quite like the feeling of not dying too.

They grin, old friends.

Sunil When's your trial?

Abdul Nobody knows. My mother's having a heart attack trying to find out.

Sunil You mean a fucking heart attack?

Abdul You've met her, then.

Sunil Do you still have to report?

Abdul 'Fraid so. I think I'm going to report as a youth for the rest of my life.

They both smile.

Sunil Well at least your family's going to be rich, aren't they?

Abdul Who told you that?

Sunil They've got a place in Annawadi. That's not a bad thing to have. From what I hear, everyone's trying to buy them up.

Abdul We've got speculators coming in, because they've heard it's going to be knocked down. Everyone's after the compensation. Anyway, why are you up so early? I thought you worked at night.

Sunil doesn't reply.

Well?

Sunil Oh, you know.

Abdul No, I don't know. Tell me.

Sunil shakes his head, embarrassed.

Sunil It got kind of tricky.

Abdul Tricky? How?

Sunil I got beaten up.

Abdul Where?

Sunil By the guards. At the airport. They shaved my head. I didn't like that. And they stripped me naked. I didn't like that either.

It's a joke, but it's not. Sunil is grave.

Abdul What are you saying? You're not a thief?

Sunil Let's just say: I'm not a thief at the minute.

Abdul No.

Sunil Not at the minute. I'm collecting rubbish. Like my father.

Abdul Good.

Sunil I'm a picker.

Abdul nods. His eyes have teared up.

It's not cos of anything you said.

Abdul looks at him.

Abdul It's not easy. I try to be ice. I try. I try not to be dirty water. I tell Allah I love him immensely, immensely. But I tell him I cannot be better because of how the world is.

Sunil is awed for a moment. Abdul reaches into his pocket and hands him coins.

Here's two rupees.

Sunil Thanks.

He pockets them.

Abdul You need to get going.

Sunil OK.

Abdul The sun's coming up, all the rubbish'll be gone in twenty minutes.

Sunil OK.

Abdul I'm just telling you. If you're going to be a picker, first thing, you have to be early.

Sunil OK, sure. But let me tell you something.

Abdul What?

Sunil When I got here, I happened to look down. Come over here, can you see? Just lean over.

Abdul has been led across to look. Sunil leans right over, Abdul does the same.

Abdul What am I looking at?

Sunil Down there. D'you see? On that shelf. Can you see?

Abdul You're joking.

Sunil This place is a taxi stand. What happens is – you can see – they throw the stuff into the river.

Abdul Sure.

Sunil D'you see? Cans? Water bottles? Only they get trapped on the ledge. There's all that stuff down there and nobody ever saw it.

They're upright again.

Abdul I think they saw it. I don't think that's the problem.

Sunil What is the problem?

Abdul Just like how you might kill yourself trying to get it.

Sunil What does that mean? You're not up for it?

Abdul puts his hands up in denial.

It's not hard, man. You just drop from the bridge.

Abdul And when you get there?

Sunil Simple. You climb back up.

Abdul laughs.

It's waiting. Look at it, Abdul. All that stuff, just waiting for someone with the courage.

Abdul reaches down and picks up a leaf from the ground. He tears the leaf into pieces. He puts the pieces on his hand, then he blows. The pieces land all over Sunil – on his head, on his face, on his clothes, like confetti.

Abdul I'll see you around.

Sunil I'll see you around, man.

Abdul goes over to his vehicle to push it away.

Take care.

Abdul disappears. Sunil is left alone on the bridge. The morning sun comes out. Once more he leans over to check. Then he gets up on the parapet. He stands for a moment, getting his balance, judging the distance to the sliver of concrete. Then he jumps.

End of Act Two.

Printed in the USA
CPSIA information can be obtained
at www.ICGtesting.com
LVHW091146150724
785511LV00005B/574

9 780865 478350